THE WRI

James Charlton is the author or co-author of twelve books and was formerly editor-in-chief at several New York publishing houses. He now heads his own book packaging company. Mr. Charlton lives in New York City and Lakeville, Connecticut.

Lisbeth Mark is a writer and former literary agent and is the author of *The Book of Hierarchies.* Ms. Mark lives in New York City.

The WRITER'S HOME COMPANION

BY
JAMES CHARLTON
&
LISBETH MARK

Penguin Books

PENGUIN BOOKS
Published by the Penguin Group
Viking Penguin Inc., 40 West 23rd Street,
New York, New York 10010, U.S.A.
Penguin Books Ltd, 27 Wrights Lane,
London W8 5TZ, England
Penguin Books Australia Ltd, Ringwood,
Victoria, Australia
Penguin Books Canada Ltd, 2801 John Street,
Markham, Ontario, Canada L3R 1B4
Penguin Books (N.Z.) Ltd, 182–190 Wairau Road,
Auckland 10, New Zealand

Penguin Books Ltd, Registered Offices:
Harmondsworth, Middlesex, England

First published in the United States of America by
Franklin Watts 1987
Published in Penguin Books 1989

1   3   5   7   9   10   8   6   4   2

THE WRITER'S HOME COMPANION
was designed by Hudson Studio
Ossining, New York,
and produced by James Charlton Associates
New York, New York

Photos and illustrations are from the following sources:
New York Public Library, Viking Penguin Inc., Dell Publishing
Company, Pocket Books Inc., and *Publishers Weekly*.

LIBRARY OF CONGRESS CATALOGING IN PUBLICATION DATA
Charlton, James, 1939–
The writer's home companion.
1. Authors—Anecdotes. I. Mark, Lisbeth. II. Title.
PN165.C36   1989   808.88'2   88–25454
ISBN 0 14 01.1012 7 (pbk.)

Printed in the United States of America by
Arcata Graphics, Kingsport, Tennessee
Set in Goudy Old Style

I MAGINE the writer at work. Sitting at a desk with a yellow pad, Remington or IBM at the ready, faced with a blank piece of paper or screen to be filled. Words quickly roll into pristine sentences filling dozens of pages peopled by brilliantly conceived characters maneuvering through a wickedly conceived plot. The perfect title comes in a predictable flash of reliable inspiration. An adoring agent holds off a hoard of eager publishers all clamoring for the right to snatch the book away from the author's long-time friend and avuncular editor and present the book to an adoring audience. Booksellers exalt and critics rave.

If you swallow that scenario you probably believe those ads with headlines that blare out, "publisher seeking to pay authors." Since the days of Alexander Pope and John Dryden the publishing trade has had little to do with reliable inspiration, inherent creativity or dependable readership. A few cynics would add that it has little to do with great writing.

Writing, truly fine writing, is one of the most difficult enterprises one can undertake. It is a singular effort, dependent on no one else during its creation. There aren't supportive collaborators as there might be with song writing, screen writing, or other creative activities. As Gene Fowler said, "Writing is easy; all you do is sit staring at a blank sheet of paper until the drops of blood form on your forehead." And every author would agree—anything is easier than writing.

The only thing more difficult than being a writer is being a happily published one. For once the book is written, the baby is born. The gestation period might have taken months or years but it is then put in the hands of someone else to care for it. Rarely does it end happily ever after. A book is a hodgepodge of ego, talent, discipline, inspiration, marketing, editing, selling, timing, rejection, loneliness and, alas, returns. Out of all those activities come frustrations, triumphs and disasters and, for our purposes, great tales.

It is only natural that the literary life would inspire a wealth of anecdotes and narratives. After all, who better than someone dealing with words and books to relate irony, wit, metaphor, the stuff of legends, or just a great story. For it is great stories that we hope you will find in these pages, tales to amuse, inform and surprise any reader. For writers there is much here to provide inspiration and solace about the waywardness of publishing.

THE WRITER'S HOME COMPANION is a collection of delightful literary vignettes for anyone interested in books, writing and the literary life. Many people were kind enough to help us with this book by providing stories, recalling incidents, and correcting or providing facts about anecdotes. We would especially like to thank the following people: Isaac Asimov, Julian Bach, Nick Bakalar, John Baker, Barbara Binswanger, Kay Boyle, Walter Bradbury, Gene Brissie, Knox Burger, Tom Congdon, John Diamond, Lucianne Goldberg, Bill Grose, Dick Grossman, Bill Henderson, Peggy and John Hooper, Harold Kuebler, Ken Lang, John D. MacDonald, Ferris Mack, Millie Marmur, Evan Marshall, Ken McCormick, Charles Newman, Betsy Nolan, Patrick O'Connor, Hank Perrine, Miriam Phelps, David Ragan, Henry Reath, Pat Strachan, Bill Thompson, Sam Vaughan and finally our editor, Ed Breslin.

THE WRITER'S HOME COMPANION

THOMAS MANN
EX·LIBRIS

*Thomas Mann's whimsical bookplate
designed by Emil Preetorius.*

THE word "book" is derived from the Anglo-Saxon/
German word for "beech." The bark of the beech tree
was the material on which ancient texts were inscribed.
James Landis named his imprint at William Morrow &
Company, Beech Tree Books.

• • •

BOOKS started looking like, well, books, in the third
century. The long sheets of parchment were folded into
more manageable "leaves," which were stitched together,
and then the covers were usually made of wood. The only
people capable of reading and writing were monks and professional scribes who copied books by hand. It would take
approximately one year to complete five copies of the Bible.
This might explain why, in the eleventh century, Ingulf, the
Abbot of Croyland, issued an edict stating, "The lending of
books, as well as the smaller without pictures as the larger
with pictures, is forbidden under the penalty of ex-
communication." Libraries were holy places, secreted away
in monasteries, and they rarely housed more than a few
dozen treasured works. Risking their loss would have, indeed, been a form of sacrilege.

• • •

IT was not until 1709 that a law was passed in England
giving an author a legal right to own his own literary
property. It was the first act of its kind anywhere in Europe.
Until that time, a monopoly, a publisher's guild called the
Stationer's Company (founded in 1534), decided what was
published and when. Every book-length work published had
to be approved by this guild. This enabled the crown to

control heretical and anti-royal material from seeing the light of print. Any book published without the approval of the Stationer's Company meant the printer could face legal charges and often did. The act passed in 1709, however, was promoted not by the writers but by the booksellers (as publishers were then called). They were the real victors because they were then free to give the writer some token payment for a manuscript for which they owned the copyright. For fourteen years, they could print or license out a work in whatever manner they chose. After fourteen years, the rights reverted to the author.

• • •

MARK Twain wrote of his publication plans for *The Adventures of Huckleberry Finn* to his business manager, publisher (and nephew), Charles L. Webster:

> Keep it diligently in mind that we don't issue until we have made a *big sale*. Get to your canvassing early and drive it with all your might. With an intent and purpose of issuing on the 10th or 15th of next December (the best time in the year to tumble a big pile into the trade); but if we haven't 40,000 subscriptions we simply postpone publication till we get them.

• • •

IN the eighteenth century, writers had only two ways of holding onto their copyrights (and their integrity). They could either find a wealthy patron (and be subject to their whims), or they could publish their manuscripts by subscription. The subscription method worked only if authors had a substantial following. A book would be announced as being in the planning stages, and interested parties would give the publisher money up front to secure a copy of the work. The added cachet was that their names would appear on the first page of the first edition, along with those of the other subscribers. For example, John Dryden sold off "shares" for his translation of Virgil and made the incredible sum of 1,200 pounds, which made him a wealthy man. Alexander Pope made 5,000 pounds in subscriptions for his translation of Homer, which made him financially independent. Although John Milton sold the copyright to *Paradise Lost* to his publisher for 10 pounds, the publisher made a small fortune publishing the masterpiece by subscription, trading on Milton's formidable popularity.

• • •

IT was James Boswell who explained, "As physicians are called 'The Faculty', and Counsellors at Law 'The Profession', the booksellers of London are called 'The Trade'."

1935   1938   1938   1942 (U.S.)

1946   1946   1947   1949

Versions of the American and British logo over the years.

• • •

PUBLISHING houses come by their names, if not those of the founding members, in many a strange manner. The name "Penguin," for example, was suggested by the founder's secretary, Joan Coles. Allen Lane was looking for a logo that would suggest "a dignified flippancy"—the overall feeling he wanted for his new list of orange-and-white-jacketed softcover books. Edward Young created the colophon by studying the penguins at the Regent's Park Zoo in London. The original name chosen for what is now known in America as Viking Penguin was to be Half-Moon Press, in honor of Henry Hudson's ship. Rockwell Kent was commissioned to design the colophon but didn't like the look of the English schooner and, instead, drew a Viking warship. The company liked the logo so much that they changed the name of the publishing house to the Viking Press.

* * *

ALLEN Lane started his Penguin Books with a capital of 100 pounds, and, naturally, had a difficult time launching the company. He set his sights on Clifford Prescott, the chief buyer for F. W. Woolworth's. However, it was Mrs. Prescott who saw the promise in the line of inexpensive editions of the popular books of the day, and she urged her husband to order thirty-four thousand copies from the first list (which included the works of Ernest Hemingway, Agatha Christie, André Maurois, and Dorothy Sayers). The first offices of the fledging company were in the crypt of Holy Trinity Church in London. The tombs were used as files, and the packers, in an effort to brighten up the surroundings, hung pinups over their work areas. The management then had to arrange for blinds, which, when required, could be pulled down to hide the nudes. The problem was that the vicar would pop in on the men to see how things were going with "the dear boys."

* * *

PLAYING a round of golf together, Andrew Carnegie turned to Frank Nelson Doubleday and asked his friend, "How much money did you make in your book business last month?" Doubleday told Carnegie that it was impossible to say—that publishers had no way to tally their profits from one month to the next. Carnegie responded, "Do you know what I would do if I were in a business in which I couldn't tell the amount of monthly profit? I would get out of it." The remarks made a "great impression" on Doubleday and on his company. Doubleday later wrote, "We immediately set to work to organize our accounting department so that we could tell our condition at the end of each month."

* * *

THE following appeared in an editorial in an 1898 edition of the *New York Times* describing the fate of paperback books purchased by travelers on the road:

> The torn cover bears the soil of the journey, and even after the story is forgotten, the book yet spells sandwiches, cinders and satchel to tired eyes as long as it lies on the table. In desperation you stick it in the bookcase, but all the world can see that it's a parvenu. The choice vellums draw away from it, the daintily bound essays and poems will have none of it, solemn history frowns on it, polite fiction scorns it, well-fed reference books turn their backs on the waif of the stations. Even the recherche travel (its fortune in leather) fails to take pity on this poor "little brother of the rich." Though you put all the paper-covered volumes on a shelf by themselves, the result is not better, for you have incorporated a little slum district in the literary community.

THE invention and improvement of machine-made paper, typesetting techniques, and faster presses helped to bring about wide-scale distribution of paperback books. The great-grandfather of the modern paperback was a series of inexpensively bound periodicals published in 1831 by the American Library of Useful Knowledge. Other publishers followed their lead until 1843, when the postal service started charging a higher book rate instead of the less expensive newspaper rate. Also, the publishers had gone head to head in a kind of price war of pirated English editions and burned themselves—and the new industry. The paperback business was reborn, however, in the 1870s, when low-cost pulp paper became available. In 1891, the International Copyright Law was passed that put an end to pirating copies of popular novels from Europe (for which the publisher paid absolutely nothing). The modern softcover publishing industry was back on track in 1939, however, when Pocket Books issued its first ten titles—selling at 25 cents each.

• • •

AN article in an 1884 issue of *Publishers Weekly* complained mightily at the cheap paperbacks pirated from Europe: "In the rage for cheapness we have sacrificed everything for slop, and a dainty bit of bookmaking is like a jewel in the swine's snout."

• • •

HENRY David Thoreau had occasion to say, in all candor, "I now have a library of nearly nine hundred volumes, over seven hundred of which I wrote myself." As it happens, the publication of Thoreau's *A Week on the Con-*

cord and Merrimack Rivers coincided with the frenzied onset of the California Gold Rush. There were fortunes sprinkled in the hills around Sacramento, and few people were interested in reading about the ethereal treasures of a New England riverbank. Thoreau recorded in his journal, "The edition was limited to one thousand copies, and eventually I had to buy most of them myself," which accounted for his uneasy boast regarding his prolificacy.

• • •

THOSE who complain that today's mammoth bookstores are impersonal supermarkets should breathe a sigh of relief that an earlier bookselling innovation never took hold. In 1946, a book-vending machine was put into operation in the subway arcade at 60 East Forty-second Street in New York City. The machine offered fifteen different pocket-sized titles at 25 cents apiece.

• • •

IZAAK Walton thought it was undignified that his publisher should stoop to paying to advertise his book *The Compleat Angler* when it was published in 1653. The ad read, "An interesting discourse on fish and fishing, not unworthy of the perusal of most anglers."

• • •

ON Christopher Morley's last novel, it was clearly specified in the contract that the publisher could not spend any money advertising the book. However, this was done as a publicity stunt and, ultimately, the author did allow the publisher to invest money in promoting the book.

A 1920's photo of a literary shrine in Mexico City's Chapultepec Park where readers could sit on benches next to statues of Don Quixote and his faithful squire Sancho Panza. Bookcases in the base of each statue contained volumes of great literature available to anyone.

GEORGE Bernard Shaw was not the least bit fond of publishers. In a letter, he wrote:

> I object to publishers: the one service they have done me is to teach me to do without them. They combine commercial rascality with artistic touchiness and pettishness, without being either good business men or fine judges of literature. All that is necessary in the production of a book is an author and a bookseller, without any intermediate parasite.

• • •

IN his journal, Samuel Butler echoed Shaw's sentiments:

> I have seen enough of my publishers to know that they have no ideas of their own about literature save what they can clutch at as believing it to be a straight tip from a business point of view. Heaven forbid that I should blame them for doing exactly what I should do myself in their place, but, things being as they are, they are no use to me. They have confidence in me and they must have this or they will do nothing for me beyond keeping my books on their shelves. Perhaps it is better that I should not have a chance of becoming a hack-writer, for I should grasp it at once if it were offered me.

• • •

ALEXANDER Pope wrote of the notoriously unscrupulous publishers of the 1700s, "What Authors lose, their Booksellers have won, / So Pimps grow rich, while Gallants undone."

T HE idea of a book club (subscribers receiving new books delivered to their doorstep by the postal service) was conceived and developed by Harry Scherman, one of the founders of the Book of the Month Club. He had started an extremely successful business in 1916 called the Little Leather Library, which was a series of pocket-sized editions of the classics. Ten years later, Scherman transferred the idea to include new titles and offered them to the public on a magazine-like subscription basis. The books were chosen by a committee made up of eminent editors, who were asked to make their selections based simply on their own enthusiasm for the books. Management had no say whatsoever. The first Book of the Month Club selection was mailed out in April 1926 to about five thousand customers. The Literary Guild started up a year later.

• • •

S IMON and Schuster published a juvenile book titled, *Dr. Dan the Bandage Man* and, at the last moment, decided to include a half dozen adhesive bandages in each book. Publisher Richard Simon had a friend at the Johnson and Johnson Company and sent him a telegram reading, "PLEASE SHIP TWO MILLION BAND-AIDS IMMEDIATELY." The following day, he received a wire back, "BAND-AIDS ON THEIR WAY. WHAT THE HELL HAPPENED TO YOU?"

D R. John Wolcot, who wrote under the pen name of
Peter Pindar, was asked to toast the health of a book-
seller with whom he was dining. Wolcot, holding a bottle of
ruby port aloft, is reported to have cried, "No! Let us drink a
bumper to our own: for this is author's blood." The poet
Thomas Campbell called publishers, "ravens, croakers,
suckers of innocent blood, and living men's brains." Campbell drank a toast to Napoleon's health one night amid
shouts of protest that an Englishman would mention of the
name of an enemy of Britain (let alone drink his health):
"But gentlemen," he retorted, "he once shot a publisher."
Napoleon, in fact, had sentenced German publisher Johann
Philipp Palm to death because he had printed subversive
material that had enraged the ruler.

• • •

T O his publisher, the infamous Jacob Tonson, John
Dryden said, "All of your trade are sharks, but since you
are no worse than others, I probably shall not leave you."

• • •

J OHN Dryden, John Milton, Sir Walter Scott, William
Thackeray, and Alexander Pope were all at the mercy of
the infamous Grubb Street booksellers, as publishers were
then called, who prided themselves on their lack of princi-
ples. The most notorious of these London booksellers was
Edmund Curll. He was known for publishing pornography
with the names of famous authors printed on the title page—
when they had no association with the books whatsoever.
He was also fond of stealing famous correspondences of the

socially prominent and issuing them in pamphlet form for the general public, as well as pirating manuscripts from his competitors and publishing them at a reduced cover price. Horace Walpole acknowledged Curll's tricks when he wrote a friend from abroad, "And then one should have that odious Curll get at one's letters, and publish them like Whitfield's Journal, or for a supplement to the Traveller's Pocket-companion."

It was Daniel Defoe who is credited with coining the word "Curllicism" to describe a crime committed by a book-seller against an author. Curll did spend some time in jail when his various "Curllicisms" caught up with him. Alexander Pope almost successfully poisoned Curll because of their mutual involvement with Lady Mary Montagu.

It was Curll who fine-tuned the practice of spinning out a "quickie" biography upon the untimely death of a famous individual. He kept a crew of hack writers he dispatched to gather gossip the moment anyone interesting died. Curll almost always won the race among the other Grubb Street booksellers with the first "authentic" behind-the-scenes story. Dr. John Arbuthnot, referring to Curll's practices, said, "Biography is one of the new terrors of death."

• • •

EDWARD Gibbon gave an unintentionally ironic review of Henry Fielding, a contemporary, reminiscent of *Ozymandias*. He wrote, "But the romance of Tom Jones, that exquisite picture of human manners, will outlive the palace of the Escorial and the Imperial Eagle of Austria." The Escorial was ravaged by fire a century later, and the Imperial Eagle of Austria took a permanent fall in 1918.

STEPHEN Crane's novel, *Maggie: A Girl of the Streets*, was rejected by the large commercial publishers of his day because they found the subject and language too harsh for the readers of 1892. The story was set in the Bowery of New York City and depicted all the horrific reality of street life. Crane decided to publish the novel himself but used the pseudonym of Johnson Smith (the two most popular names in the telephone book) to protect his job as a newspaper reporter. The book sold only one hundred copies and Crane, having spent his savings on the venture, was forced to use the unsold copies to fuel the furnace that winter. Miraculously, William Dean Howells had a copy brought to his attention, and he was instrumental in getting Crane's classic, *The Red Badge of Courage*, published three years later. *Maggie*, too, was then rereleased and received enthusiastically.

• • •

EVEN though his statue now graces university property, Percy Bysshe Shelley was expelled from Oxford when he self-published *Necessities for Atheism*—a title he deliberately chose to be provocative and, therefore, sell copies. While the owners of an Oxford bookshop were having lunch, Shelley convinced the shopclerks to try to sell as many copies as possible in the time allotted—at 6 pence each. Shelley could not resist helping the book along and tossed copies into the shop window. A reverend, passing the display, caught sight of the outrageous title and, when the owners returned, brought it to their attention in no uncertain terms. The copies of Shelley's publishing experiment were burned in the kitchen at the back of the shop.

UPTON Sinclair's *The Jungle*, was turned down by publisher after publisher for being too violent. With Jack London's help, Sinclair went about selling subscriptions (much like his literary ancestors, John Dryden and Alexander Pope) for $1.20, raising over $4,000 to subsidize the first printing of the book. This was more money than he had earned in five years of being a writer. The publishing company, Doubleday and Page, eventually bought the manuscript and published a second first edition simultaneously with Sinclair's own.

• • •

WITH the windfall he earned from his best-selling novel, *The Jungle*, Upton Sinclair founded the Helicon House Colony in Englewood, New Jersey, in 1909. The settlement offered shelter for political activists and writers, and was run along socialistic lines. Sinclair made a run for a New Jersey congressional seat (and three decades later, the governorship of California) during this period. A janitor at the Helicon House Colony was the as yet unpublished Sinclair Lewis.

• • •

THE self-publication of Thomas Paine's pamphlet, based upon his experiences titled, "The Case of the Offices of Excise," got him fired. Paine decided to follow the lead of many other dissatisfied young men of his day and left for the as yet un-United States. In January 1776, he self-published a tract that was to set off fireworks more far-reaching than anyone could have imagined—Paine's *Common Sense*. The first printing sold out in two weeks (one thousand copies, priced at 2 shillings each, forty-seven pages in length). The printer, Robert Bell, decided to issue another edition (with some new material added) without Paine's permission or foreknowledge. Although the pamphlet eventually sold well over five hundred thousand copies in the newly declared United States of America and throughout the world, Paine said he never made a single penny from the pamphlet credited with inspiring the Declaration of Independence. He did see to it, however, that Bell kept the cover price to 1 shilling so that everyone could afford it.

· · ·

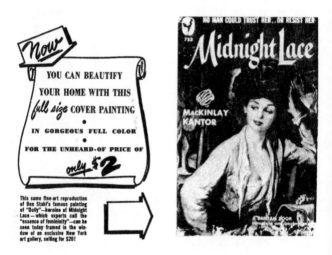

A 1951 ad for a Bantam book and print of the cover art.

SAMUEL Butler wrote about the perils of self-publishing in his *Notebooks*:

> I was too lazy to go about from publisher to publisher. . . . I found publishers' antechambers so little to my taste that I soon tired and fell back on the short and easy method of publishing my book myself. Of course, therefore, it failed to sell. I know more about these things now, and will never publish a book at my own risk again, or at any rate I will send somebody else round the antechambers with it for a good while before I pay for publishing it.

The author was describing what was to become known as a literary agent.

• • •

WALT Whitman self-published the first editions of *Leaves of Grass*, wrote his own reviews (describing himself "of pure American breed, large and lusty, a naive, masculine, affectionate, contemplative, sensual, imperious person"), and even delivered the books himself from a great basket he hand-carried to his subscribers. It was not until Whitman published his sixth edition in 1876, with Emerson's endorsement and with Whitman's British publisher, W. M. Rosseti, championing the volume in England, that the book became an international best-seller. Whitman printed his sixth edition in a fine leather binding in honor of the nation's centennial and sold the copies from his basket for $5 dollars each.

EDGAR Allan Poe opted to self-publish *Tamerlane and Other Poems*. He was able to sell only forty copies and made less than a dollar after expenses. Ironically, a century later, one of his self-published copies sold at auction for over $11,000.

• • •

THERE are as many stories about famous manuscripts being rejected as there are famous manuscripts accepted on the first submission. The James Joyce's *Dubliners*, for example, was rejected twenty-two times before it found a home, while J. P. Donleavy's novel, *The Ginger Man*, was turned down thirty-six times. The novel, *Cool Hand Luke*, by Donn Pearce, was turned down by forty-nine editors before it turned up on the "slushpile" at Fawcett. The first reader, Larry Fleischer, scribbled "a good book" on the covering letter and passed it along for another reading. The editors agreed and enlisted Scribner's to publish the hardcover edition. The movie rights were sold, and Pearce's career was launched.

• • •

IRVING Stone, who virtually invented the biographical novel, had his first manuscript rejected by twenty-six publishers before it was finally accepted for publication by Longmans Green. Stone received an advance of $500 for his novel based upon the life of Vincent Van Gogh. With the demise of Longmans Green, Doubleday and Company took over the book. They had been one of the twenty-six to turn down the novel during the first go-around, and buried in the files was a long-forgotten reader's report that stated, "*Lust for Life*, by I. Stone. A long, dull novel about an artist."

The winner of the costume contest at the 1921 American Booksellers Association costume ball where everyone had to come dressed as a title published that year. The winner, a buyer from Macy's, came dressed as H. G. Wells's Outline of History, *beating out* Raggedy Ann *also published that year.*

RECENTLY returned from service in World War II, James Michener was working as a textbook editor at Macmillan Publishing Company. He wrote a book of connected short stories based upon his wartime experiences. Macmillan published the collection in 1947, but the book had only a small sale. Meanwhile, Michener had made another submission to Macmillan—this time a novel. Editor George Brett called the young employee into his office and suggested Michener forget about writing and stick to editing. Yes, they would publish it, but hereafter, as a matter of policy, Macmillan would follow a trade practice and not publish the works of employees. Michener called on Saxe Commins, an editor at Random House, and Commins agreed to publish the novel, titled, *The Fires of Spring.* Eleven days after the contract was signed, the collection, *Tales from the South Pacific* was awarded the Pulitzer Prize, and Michener was an overnight literary sensation. Macmillan never did publish another one of his books.

• • •

A COLUMNIST with the *London Financial Times* declared the following to be a genuine rejection letter from a Chinese economic journal:

> We have read your manuscript with boundless delight. If we were to publish your paper, it would be impossible for us to publish any work of a lower standard. And as it is unthinkable that in the next thousand years we shall see its equal, we are, to our regret, compelled to return your divine composition, and to beg you a thousand times to overlook our short sight and timidity.

PUBLISHER John Farrar once wrote:

> The question of rejections and their handling is a troublesome one. Printed rejections, post cards, and letters are used by many publishers for many manuscripts. Editors write most carefully to any author who shows promise. It is considered by some unfair to criticize a manuscript in a letter of rejection unless there is a strong possibility that the publisher would seriously consider a revised manuscript. However, when a publisher writes a gracious letter of rejection and says that he would like to see more of an author's work, he usually means it. Many authors feel that they do not get fair treatment from publishers. I think they are mistaken, but I have never found a way of persuading them of that fact.

• • •

AFTER its successful publication in England, Harper and Brothers bought the American rights to Henry James's *The Ambassadors*. The novel was praised for its brilliant structure when it was first released in the United States in 1903. James, a tinkerer, could not resist changing a few words when the second edition was being readied for the printer. However, no one—not the publishers, the public, nor the author himself—noticed that chapter 29 preceded chapter 28. It was not until 1950 that Robert E. Young, a literary critic, noticed the error. He wrote a paper about his discovery and so influenced the publisher to reissue the novel in 1955, with the chapters placed in their proper order. Amid much publicity, *The Ambassadors* was republished. However, the two chapters were still inversed. Harper and Brothers went back to the printer, and a properly chaptered edition was published here, at last.

• • •

MARK Twain's American classic, *The Adventures of Huckleberry Finn*, was scheduled for publication months before it was actually released. The book was delayed when it was discovered that an engraving of the character Silas Phelps had been altered. A mysterious "artist" had sketched in an anatomically correct "addition" that gave a very different twist to the caption reading, "Who do you reckon it is?" Two hundred fifty copies had to be recalled (and were, to a copy, retrieved successfully), making the British edition of this all-American classic three days older than its American counterpart. The *New York Herald Tribune* carried a notice from publisher Charles Webster promising a $500 reward for the apprehension and conviction of the person,

> who so altered an engraving in *Huckleberry Finn* as to make it obnoxious. . . . By the punch of an awl or graver, the illustration became an immoral one. . . . Had the first edition been run off, our loss would have been $25,000. Had the mistake not been discovered, Mr. Clemens' [Mark Twain was the pseudonym of Samuel Clemens] credit for decency and morality would have been destroyed.

No one ever took responsibility, and the book went on to become an international classic.

IN the early 1920s, Mr. Hodder, of London's prestigious old house Hodder and Stoughton, barreled into the office of his grandson with a copy of Dulac's *Rubaiyat of Omar Khayyam* in his shaking hand. "Ernest, what is this pagan book you have dared to publish over my imprint?" Hodder demanded. J. E. H. W. replied, "Why, Grandad, that is one of the greatest classics of all time." Hodder pronounced, "Classic or no classic, I will not tolerate the publication of such heathen rubbish!"

Defending the publication, J. E. H. W. said, "Grandad, it is beautifully illustrated by one of the greatest artists of our day—it is a proud publication." Hodder was not to be mollified. "The artist only abets the author," he maintained, "whoever he is, in the presentation of a purely pagan and disgusting book. I will have none of it." The young man tried desperately to arrive at some acceptable defense of the book and, ultimately, found it. Falling back on what he had learned at the knee of three generations of publishing wizards, he quietly pointed out, "But, Grandad, we made a profit of 800 pounds on that book in the last twelve months." The rage disappeared in the old man's face and his characteristic smile returned. He patted his grandson on the shoulder and cautioned him, "You will be careful, Ernest, my boy. Won't you?"

R ESEARCHING a biography of Dorothy Parker, Marion
  Meade wrote to Norton asking for permission to review
any files it had from Parker's publisher, Boni and Liveright.
Norton had purchased their backlist many years before.
Norton wrote back to Meade, saying they did not have any
files of Parker's correspondences with her former publisher.
Meade was contacted some time later by Norton, saying she
could go through what there was. Opening the first file,
Meade found her original letter stapled to a copy of Norton's
reply saying no such file existed.

• • •

A NUMBER of publishing houses, such as McGraw-Hill
  and World Publishing, initiated a royalty payout plan
for a few of their successful authors. The arrangements var-
ied, but all were done to help the author defer taxes on
earned royalty.

Doubleday was among these publishers, and they had
two plans: one a boilerplate clause available to every author,
and another slightly different plan offered to only a few of
their most successful authors. Both arrangements allowed
Doubleday to pay a fixed yearly amount, which was selected
by the author, no matter what the royalty earnings were,
with the balance to be invested by the publisher.

The young Stephen King was offered this plan and
opted for an annual payment of $50,000, seemingly a prince-
ly sum, but his kitty soon swelled to over $3 million. Realiz-
ing that, at $50,000 a year, his Doubleday income would
outlast him (William Holden faced a similar situation in his
earnings from the film *The Bridge Over the River Kwai*) King,
no longer a Doubleday author, asked to have the agreement

ended and a lump sum payment made. Doubleday refused, saying that if it ended the agreement without "a due consideration," the IRS would conclude that all such agreements could be easily terminated. Doubleday wanted something of value in exchange and asked for two books from the author. Instead he delivered one novel, *Pet Sematary* (with a first printing of five hundred thousand copies), and with that King was out of his contract.

• • •

JONATHAN Swift summed up editorial work as follows:

> *Blot out, correct, insert, refine,*
> *Enlarge, diminish, interline;*
> *Be mindful, when invention fails,*
> *To scratch your head, and bite your nails.*

• • •

A 1931 bookmobile.

I N the first months of 1776, a committee was established to review Thomas Jefferson's early drafts of the Declaration of Independence. Jefferson, proud of his work, was resisting having his pride and joy edited until Benjamin Franklin took the matter in hand. He told his colleague the story of John Thompson, a hatter, who was about to open his first shop. The young entrepreneur designed a sign to hang outside his business to attract customers. He wrote, "John Thompson, hatter, makes and sells hats for ready money," and proudly showed his work to his friends and asked their opinions, confident they would unanimously approve. They pointed out that "hatter" was not necessary because the sign specified that he made and sold hats. "Makes" could be dropped because customers did not need to know who actually created the hats but that they were, simply, available. One friend pointed out that the town did not accept credit and so the phrase, "for ready money" was not required. This left "John Thompson sells hats." It was decided that specifying "sells" was extraneous because it was not expected the hats would be given away. A large picture of a hat canceled the need for that word, too. This reduced the sign to just the name of the proprietor—John Thompson—and the picture of the hat. Franklin's clever illustration was accepted by Jefferson, who in turn accepted the editorial suggestions of the committee.

• • •

D. H. Lawrence told Aldous Huxley he rarely corrected or edited what he had written. He claimed that he was "incapable" of correcting. If he was dissatisfied with what he had written, he preferred to rewrite the entire work (as he did with *Lady Chatterly's Lover*). Thornton Wilder echoed F. Scott Fitzgerald's definition of his "notebook" when he wrote, "I constantly rewrite, discard and replace the cycle of plays. Some are on the stove, some are in the oven, some are in the waste-basket. There are no first drafts in my life. An incinerator is a writer's best friend."

• • •

WRITERS have their own methods for rewriting. Gore Vidal never reread the manuscript on which he was working until he had completed the first draft. He claimed it was too discouraging otherwise. Philip Roth says it sometimes takes him six months to produce what he considers an acceptable page. Truman Capote reviewed what he had written in longhand at the end of every productive day and made his changes on the spot. He liked to write two versions of everything—the first on yellow paper and the second on white. Once he had the story where he wanted it, he typed it up (making any final touchups on the typewriter) and after that rarely changed a word. Raymond Carver professed to look forward to polishing his stories. "It's something I love to do, putting words in and taking words out." Carver routinely wrote twenty to thirty drafts of a story and forty or fifty of a poem.

Reading over the manuscripts of Robert Browning's poetry, Robert Louis Stevenson commented, "He floods acres of paper with brackets and inverted commas."

IAN Fleming sent a copy of his James Bond novel, titled *Dr. No*, to his friend, Noel Coward. Coward wrote back:

> Your descriptive passages, as usual, are very good indeed. . . . I am willing to accept the centipede, the tarantulas, the land crabs, the giant squid. . . . I am even willing to forgive your reckless use of inverted verbs—"I inch, Thou inches, He snakes, I snake, We palp, They palp", etc. but what I will neither accept nor forgive is the highly inaccurate statement that when it is eleven A.M. in Jamaica, it is six A.M. in dear old England. This, dear boy, to put not too fine a point on it, is a f—— lie. When it is eleven A.M. in Jamaica, it is *four* P.M. in dear old England, and it is carelessness of this kind that makes my eyes steel slits of blue.

• • •

RECALLING F. Scott Fitzgerald's remark to Thomas Wolfe that Fitzgerald was a "taker-outer," while Wolfe was more of a "putter-inner," James Thurber said he was with Fitzgerald. Thurber said:

> I don't believe, as Wolfe did, that you have to turn out a massive work before being judged a writer. Wolfe once told me at a cocktail party I didn't know what it was to be a writer. My wife, standing next to me, complained that, "But my husband *is* a writer," she said. Wolfe was genuinely surprised. "He is?" he asked. "Why, all I ever see is that stuff of his in *The New Yorker*."

E. M. Forster was taken by Laurence Sterne's editorial selectivity. Of *Tristram Shandy*, Forster remarked, "How did he discover the art of leaving out what he did not want to say? And why was it lost again until our own time? Can nothing liberate English fiction from conscientiousness?"

• • •

IN the late 1960s, the tremulous-voiced singer Tiny Tim was signed up by packager Jeremy P. Tarcher to write a book. The "entertainer" was paid $60,000. Months later, the finished manuscript came in; it came to a grand total of fifty-six words. Editor Ferris Mack published the manuscript without a single editorial change in the text.

• • •

Knopf salesmen in the 20's dressed like French artists, advertising books on signboards in New York's theater district.

AFTER dinner one summer night, John Keats decided to spend a contemplative hour in his garden, watching a nest of nightingales. His friend and houseguest, Charles Armitage Brown, noticed the poet return to the house holding a handful of paper strips on which Keats had scribbled indecipherable notes. He walked over to his bookcase and jammed the slips into the shelves and walked away. Intrigued, Brown retrieved the paper strips and tried to read them. He asked Keats to sit down with him and arrange the lines into stanzas. The result was *Ode to a Nightingale*. Brown then made a thorough search of Keats's library and found hundreds of similar strips of fragmented poetry. That night, he exacted a promise from Keats that Brown would be permitted to collect the strips, copy the contents, and keep track of the poet's work. Keats reluctantly agreed.

• • •

ON January 12, 1848, Charlotte Bronte wrote to G. H. Lewes:

> When authors write best, or, at least, when they write most fluently, an influence seems to waken in them, which becomes their master—which will have its own way—putting out of view all behests but its own, dictating certain words, and insisting on their own being used, whether vehement or measured in their nature; new-molding characters, giving unthought-of turns of incidents, rejecting carefully elaborated old ideas, and suddenly creating and adopting new ones.

This is from the woman who created the character of Rochester—the sister of the creator of Heathcliff.

J AMES Joyce attempted dictating parts of *Finnegan's Wake* to his protege, Samuel Beckett. It did not go as well as Joyce had hoped, and he eventually abandoned the practice. During one session, Beckett was reverently taking down every word uttered by Joyce when there was a knock at the door, and Joyce said, "Come in." Later, when Beckett was reading back what he had taken down, he repeated "come in" in the middle of a sentence. Joyce, baffled, wanted to know why Beckett had written that in, and Beckett replied, "Yes, you said that." Joyce thought it over and let it stand.

• • •

M ARK Twain had never been a great admirer of James Fenimore Cooper. He railed against his writing ability. He wrote, "In one place in the *Deerslayer,* and in the restricted space of two thirds of a page, Cooper has scored 114 offences against literary art out of a possible 115. It breaks the record." Twain also blasted Cooper's Leatherstocking series, writing:

> Every time a Cooper person is in peril, and absolute silence is worth four dollars a minute, he is sure to step on a dry twig. There may be a hundred handier things to step on, but that wouldn't satisfy Cooper. Cooper requires him to turn out and find a dry twig; and if he can't do it, go and borrow one. In fact, the Leatherstocking series ought to have been called the Broken Twig series.

C. P. Snow was one of those writers who preferred not to dedicate his books to anyone and was, therefore, shocked to receive an American edition of his book, *A Coat of Varnish*, with a dedication to Kate Marsh. He telephoned his American publisher, Charles Scribner III, and demanded to know who Kate Marsh was. Scribner went to his father and asked about the problem. "If his lordship doesn't remember to whom he dedicated his books, how should we know?" The mystery was finally solved when it was discovered that Kate Marsh was the secretary of Snow's London agent. When the British printers had sent the manuscript to the agent's office, they addressed it "To Kate Marsh," which was then incorporated by the American printers when the manuscript went to press. Scribner later said, "We thought it was very funny, but Lord Snow was not amused."

• • •

JOHN Cheever had his own special definition of a good editor: "A man I think charming, who sends me large checks, praises my work, my physical beauty, and my sexual prowess, and who has a stranglehold on the publisher and the bank."

• • •

STEPHEN King sent his first novel to the editor of the suspense novel *The Parallax View*. William G. Thompson rejected that first submission and several subsequent manuscripts until King sent along *Carrie*. Years later, some of those earlier projects were published under King's pseudonym, Richard Bachman, and one was affectionately dedicated to "W.G.T."

WILLIAM Styron worked as an editorial assistant for McGraw-Hill in 1947 and "was forced to plow my way daily through fiction and nonfiction of the humblest quality." One manuscript he rejected with a reader's report stating, "The idea of men adrift on a raft does have a certain appeal, but for the most part this is a long, solemn and tedious Pacific voyage." The book was eventually published in the United States by Rand McNally in 1950 and was titled *The Kon-Tiki Expedition,* by Thor Heyerdahl. Years later, Styron said, "Watching this book remain first on the best-seller list for unbelievable week after week, I was able to rationalize my blindness saying that if McGraw-Hill had paid me more than 90 cents an hour I might have been more sensitive to the nexus between good books and filthy lucre."

• • •

WHEN his novel, *From Here to Eternity,* was published, James Jones kept handy sealed envelopes containing 67 cents each. The "pocket" change represented the royalty he received on each book. He would give an envelope to friends who purchased the book, saying he did not want to make money on their loyalty.

SIMON and Schuster turned down Judith Krantz's novel, *Scruples*, saying it was overly plotted and suffered from too many characters. Crown Publishers bought it for a $50,000 advance and later sold off the paperback rights in an auction for half a million dollars. *Princess Daisy* set a long-standing record when Crown auctioned off those paperback rights, selling in the end to Bantam Books for $3.2 million dollars. This knocked Mario Puzo's old record of $2.5 million out of the first-place slot. *Princess Daisy* ended up earning some $5 million in various subsidiary rights sales three months before it was published .

• • •

MARGARET Mitchell's *Gone with the Wind* was "discovered" by H. L. Latham, who was in Atlanta, Georgia, on a scouting expedition, looking for new writers to sign up at Macmillan. The editor had been tipped off to seek out Margaret Mitchell, a former feature writer for the Sunday magazine of the *Atlanta Journal*. Mitchell was at first reluctant to show anyone her novel but relented. Latham remembers her sitting in his hotel lobby, "a tiny woman sitting on the divan, and beside her the biggest manuscript I had ever seen, towering two stacks almost up to her shoulders."

Latham was not enamored of the title, *Tomorrow Is Another Day*, nor of the heroine's name, which was Pansy. Retitled *Gone with the Wind* and the heroine now named Scarlett O'Hara, the novel was published by Macmillan in 1936 with a first printing of 10,000 copies. A publicist was hired to help organize a book signing at Davison's Department Store (now Macy's) in Atlanta. The publicist advised, "a small party in the book department, run a small ad in the newspaper and let her autograph her book if anyone comes."

The novel sprang onto the best-seller list and remained there two years running. The book had sold over 1 million copies at the end of 1936—which included a single order from Macy's for 50,000. The book still sells about 250,000 copies a year in the United States and 100,000 around the world. By 1983, there were more than 185 editions in print, and 25 million copies had been sold in 37 languages in 37 countries. David O. Selznick bought the film rights for $50,000.

• • •

JOHN F. Kennedy's *Profiles in Courage* is the only book to hit the best-seller lists three separate times: on publication, after the 1960 presidential elections, and after the 1963 assassination.

• • •

AFTER his book had been out for several weeks, Herman Melville wrote to Mrs. Nathaniel Hawthorne of *Moby Dick*:

> I had some vague idea while writing it, that the whole book was susceptible of an allegorical construction, and also that parts of it were—but the speciality of many of the particular subordinate allegories were first revealed to me after reading Mr. Hawthorne's letter, which, without citing any particular examples, yet intimated the part-and-parcel allegoricalness of the whale.

HARRIET Beecher Stowe's *Uncle Tom's Cabin* was one of the great literary phenomena of the nineteenth century. In the United States, 305,000 copies were sold in the year it was published, 1852. Inspired by a pamphlet Stowe had read written by Josiah Henson, a former slave, *Uncle Tom's Cabin* was the first American novel to sell over a million copies. The foreign editions accounted for another two and one half million copies.

• • •

THE most successful television/book tie-in was Alex Haley's novel, *Roots*, in 1976. As an estimated one hundred million tuned into the miniseries, hardcover sales of the book soared over the one million mark. The book was selling so rapidly that the publisher, Doubleday and Company, was forced for a time to fill orders with the smaller-sized Literary Guild edition. By early 1979, hardcover and softcover sales had reached nearly six million copies.

• • •

JACK London said bluntly that he "wrote for no other purpose than to add to the beauty that now belongs to me. I write a book for no other reason than to add three or four hundred acres to my magnificent estate."

• • •

PUBLISHER Howard Kaminsky has a unique way of describing a book for which his publishing house had high hopes: "We brought the book out at a time when the fiction list was very strong. It's always a question of how many perennial bestsellers are coming out of a given season.

It's easier to swim in a lake than in heavy surf, and this book was published somewhere near Maui."

• • •

EDMUND Spenser was in the enviable position of being a court favorite of Queen Elizabeth I. He was awarded 100 pounds by her decree upon his recitation of his poetry. The lord treasurer balked at the sum and decided it was too generous. The poet waited for nine months for the money, which never came. He opted to bring the matter to the attention of the Queen in his own way. He wrote:

> I was promised on a time
> To have reason for my rhyme;
> From that time unto this season,
> I have received not rhyme nor reason.

The Queen called up the lord treasurer and had him pay Spenser while she was in attendance, to assure no further oversights.

• • •

WINSTON Churchill, H. G. Wells, and George Bernard Shaw all received letters dated March 23, 1913, asking the same question: how much they were paid for "their stuff." The letters were signed with sincere wishes by Jack London.

• • •

NATHANIEL Hawthorne said, "The only sensible ends of literature are, first, the pleasurable toil of writing; second, the gratification of one's family and friends; and, lastly, the solid cash."

OF earning a living as a writer, Judith Krantz said, "I'm no Joan Didion—There are no intelligent, unhappy people in my books. I want to be known as a writer of good, entertaining narrative. I'm not trying to be taken seriously by the East Coast literary establishment. But I'm taken *very* seriously by the bankers."

• • •

IN an effort to keep their author's head above financial water and, therefore, free to devote his time to fulfilling his contracts, Sherwood Anderson's publisher sent him weekly checks. He ended up returning them uncashed a few weeks later saying, "It's no use. I find it impossible to work with security staring me in the face."

Perhaps with more appropriateness than writers care to contemplate, the model for the head of the Liberty dime was a poet's wife—Mrs. Wallace Stevens.

• • •

ERLE Stanley Gardner honed his story-telling skills working for pulp magazines, producing at his peak some two hundred thousand words every month. Because he was paid by the word, he wrote for length rather than literary beauty. He was famous for killing off the bad guys, using the last bullet in the hero-detective's revolver. His editor once teased Gardner by saying his characters were all such bad shots. Gardner responded, "At three cents a word, every time I say 'bang' in the story I get three cents. If you think I'm going to finish the gun battle while my hero has got fifteen cents worth of unexploded ammunition in his gun, you're nuts."

MARK Twain similarly noted, "I never write 'metropolis' for seven cents because I can get the same price for 'city.' I never write 'policeman' because I can get the same money for 'cop.'"

. . .

HARPER'S *Magazine* sent out a questionnaire to several prominent men asking things such as, "During what activity, situation, moment, or series of moments do you feel most masculine?" The responses were intriguing, and the editors decided, for a twist, to ask the same question of a group of equally prominent women. One of those was Lillian Hellman, who answered that question, "It makes me feel masculine to tell you that I do not answer questions like this without being paid for answering them."

. . .

THEODORE Dreiser had a reputation for being very careful with his money. Sailing home from Europe, he was given the option of traveling by a steamer, the *Kroonland*, or indulging himself on a brand new luxury ship equipped with every extravagance. Dreiser decided on the *Kroonland* and sailed April 1912, foregoing the opportunity to be a passenger on the maiden voyage of the *Titanic*.

. . .

MARK Twain published *The Adventures of Huckleberry Finn* at the same time he was bringing out the hottest property of his day. After months of volatile negotiations, Twain signed up the memoirs of Ulysses S. Grant. He fussed over the book to the point of ignoring his own. The attention worked because on February 27, 1886, Twain handed Grant's widow the first royalty check representing the book's earnings—$200,000. This was the biggest royalty check for decades to come. The book outsold *Huck Finn* three to one. (Robert E. Lee was also approached about doing his memoirs, but he refused, saying he had no interest making money off the blood of his men.)

• • •

IN 1751, Henry Fielding sold his novel *Amelia* to a publisher for 800 pounds. (He had sold his first manuscript, *Joseph Andrews*, for 18 pounds and 11 pence.) The publisher, Andrew Millar, was banking on the phenomenal success of Fielding's previous novel, *The History of Tom Jones, a Foundling*. He gambled on an unusually large print run and then took a finished copy to a friend, who proclaimed the novel not nearly as interesting as *Tom Jones*. The publisher panicked, fearing he would be stuck with boxes of unsold copies of the novel. Then he hit upon an idea. As was the custom, publishers would auction off unsold stock to bookstore owners. "Gentlemen," he bluffed, "I have several works to put up, for which I shall be glad if you will bid. But as to *Amelia*, every copy is bespoke." The bluff worked because the men started a delirious bidding war, competing for the "bespoken" copies. Millar sold every copy that afternoon.

• • •

SIR James M. Barrie overheard Sylvia Llewelyn-Davies warn her young son to stop eating so much candy or he would pay for it the next day. The boy replied, stuffing more chocolates in as he spoke, "I shall be sick tonight." Sir Barrie was so taken with the child's comeback that he incorporated that very scene in *Peter Pan* and subsequently paid the real author of the remark a copyright fee of a half-penny every time the play was performed.

• • •

The four and ace of Books from Jost Amman's deck of medieval playing cards.

RUDYARD Kipling once visited his publisher and close friend, F. N. Doubleday (whom Kipling called Effendi from his initials). Kipling spent part of the day on the publisher's Long Island estate entertaining Doubleday's son. He amused the young Nelson with stories about how the monkey got his tail and the leopard his spots. The young future publisher suggested Kipling write up the collection, and the *Just So* stories were born. Kipling rewarded Nelson with a penny royalty on every copy sold. The collection remains in print, still earning the penny royalty for Nelson Doubleday's children. Nelson, Junior, splits the legacy with his sister Neltje—totaling anywhere from 15 cents to $4 each year.

• • •

ANOTHER example of someone other than the writer earning royalties on a celebrated book involves James Joyce's *Ulysses*. Because the book had been declared obscene and banned in the United States, it was considered de rigueur for tourists returning from Paris in the 1930s to bring in a copy of the $10 pale-blue paperback. Publisher Bennett Cerf was certain he could change the minds of the courts and so met with the author in Paris and eventually bought the American rights for a $1,500 advance. Cerf then engaged the legal services of Morris Ernst, a well-known lawyer, to plead the case in New York. Cerf offered to pay him all the court costs. "If you win the case," he also promised, "you'll get a royalty on *Ulysses* for the rest of your life."

To ensure that the literary opinions of the book were entered in the court records, Random House instructed an employee to go to Europe and return with a copy of the book.

He docked in New York on one of the hottest days on record. The customs agents were flagging everyone to just pass by the inspection desk, but the employee argued he *wanted* to be searched. The unamused official complied and found the copy of the banned book. He refused to acknowledge it, saying, "Everybody brings that in. . . . We don't pay any attention to it." The employee demanded that the book be confiscated. The book was finally seized, and that copy was entered in evidence at the landmark trial. After two days in front of Judge Woolsey, the decision was handed down concluding that the book was not obscene. Judge Woolsey noted that the author's "locale was Celtic and his season spring" and that, though the effect in some places was "somewhat emetic, nowhere does it tend to be an aphrodisiac." Morris Ernst's law firm has been earning a royalty on the book ever since.

· · ·

IT was Richard Simon of Simon and Schuster who instituted the policy of allowing bookstores to return unsold copies of books for full credit. He came to regret that offer. Although bookstores rewarded the publisher by displaying Simon and Schuster books in their windows and on their shelves, this forced all other publishers to follow suit. Two years after the return policy went into effect, Simon scrawled, "Bookstore returns too high" across the margin of that year's financial statement. The return figure was 3 percent. Today, with the policy a publishing mainstay, returns average 25 percent at the trade houses and up to 50 percent and higher at the mass market paperback houses. One title, *Cruel Shoes*, by the comedian Steve Martin, had a 93 percent return rate when it was published in softcover by Warner Books.

• • •

THE English courts, passing judgment on Radclyffe Hall's book, *The Well of Loneliness*, admitted it was well written, but Magistrate Sir Charles Biron cautioned, "It must appear to everyone of intelligence that the better an obscene book is written, the greater is the public to whom it is likely to appeal. The more palatable the poison, the more insidious it is." Alfred A. Knopf Publishers here decided to cancel its plans to bring the book out in the United States.

• • •

BOWING to pressure and concerned about the immorality of *Sister Carrie*, the new publisher of Doubleday, Page and Company recalled the book from the stores shortly after its publication in 1900. A total of 456 copies were sold, earning the author, Theodore Dreiser, a total of $68.40 in royalties. The novel was republished in a new edition in 1952 by Doubleday and Company, the editor and Dreiser's widow having restored some thirty-six thousand words that had been removed from the first edition.

• • •

WHEN Kathleen Windsor's bawdy novel, *Forever Amber*, was banned in Boston (and the rest of Massachusetts) a full two years after it was published, the state's attorney general, George Rowell, contended that the book was obscene and that bookstores carrying it were liable for criminal action. The well-minded prosecutor came up with the following analysis of the book:

- 70 references to sexual intercourse
- 39 references to illegitimate pregnancies
- 7 abortions
- 10 descriptions of women dressing or undressing in the presence of men
- 5 references to incest and 10 to the badger game
- 13 [references] ridiculing marriage
- 49 "miscellaneous objectional passages"

Rowell ended his review of the novel by stating, "The references to women's bosoms and other parts of their anatomy were so numerous I did not even attempt to count them." The banning was eventually repealed but did help propel the sales of *Forever Amber* upward of two million copies.

OLIVER Goldsmith was forever having trouble with his creditors. Dr. Jonson rescued him from being tossed into a debtor's prison in 1764, however, and the two became lifelong friends. Jonson tells the story:

> I received one morning a message from poor Goldsmith that he was in great distress, and, as it was not in his power to come to me, begging that I would come to him directly. I sent him a guinea, and promised to come to him directly. I accordingly went as soon as I was dressed, and found that his landlady had arrested him for his rent, at which he was in a violent passion. I perceived that he had already changed my guinea and had got a bottle of Madeira and a glass before him. I put a cork into the bottle, desired he would be calm, and began to talk to him of the means by which he might be extricated. He then told me that he had a novel ready for the press, which he produced to me. I looked into it, and saw its merit; told the landlady I should soon return; and, having gone to a bookseller, sold it for 60 pounds. I brought Goldsmith the money, and he discharged his rent, not without rating his landlady in high tone for having used him so ill.

The book was Goldsmith's novel, *The Vicar of Wakefield*, and was published two years later by publisher John Newbery.

I T is thought the first novel ever to be serialized was Daniel Defoe's *Robinson Crusoe*. It was a pirated installment and appeared in the original *London Post* on October 7, 1719. The novels of Henry Fielding, William Makepeace Thackeray, and Charles Dickens were written for publication in parts and published in serial form. As Ford Madox Ford pointed out, "At the end of every part must come the Strong Situation, to keep the Plot in the reader's head until the First of Next Month."

When the first monthly installment of Dickens's *Posthumous Papers of the Pickwick Club* was published in 1836, the print run was four hundred copies. By the time the fifteenth installment was published, the print run had leaped to forty thousand copies.

There is a famous story about Dickens's *The Old Curiosity Shop*, which was being printed in serial form in a London magazine. When the ship carrying the final installment of the novel docked in New York harbor, thousands of people were said to have lined the wharves, crying out to anyone on board, "Did Little Nell die?"

• • •

F ED up with the continual requests to lend his name or a word of praise to a newly published book, Edmund Wilson had printed up postcards that read:

> Edmund Wilson regrets that it is impossible for him to: Read manuscripts, write articles or books to order, write forewords or introductions, make statements for publicity purposes, do any kind of editorial work, judge literary contests, give interviews, take part in writers'

conferences, answer questionnaires, contribute to or take any part in symposiums or "panels" of any kind, contribute manuscripts for sale, donate copies of his books to libraries, autograph works for strangers, allow his name to be used on letterheads, supply personal information about himself, supply opinions on literary or other subjects.

The thought behind the postcard backfired, however, because people started writing him letters just to get one of the famous writer's famous cards.

• • •

CHARLES Dickens once proclaimed, "There are books of which the backs and covers are by far the best parts." It was Lewis Carroll who first suggested to his publisher that the dust jacket carry the title of the book. This made Carroll's *The Hunting of the Snark* the first book to be published with a printed jacket.

Like its literary older brother *Tom Sawyer*, *The Adventures of Huckleberry Finn* was made available to the reading public in cloth and a selection of different, ornately tooled leather bindings. The subscriber could select either blue or green leather. Most chose green, making blue first editions of Mark Twain's works very rare.

• • •

"THE most unique book in the whole world" was reported to be for sale in an antique store in Paris in December 1925. What made the book so extraordinary was not the contents but the binding. In the center of the front cover was a butterfly with its wings extended, each wing measuring about one inch. According to a description sheet accompanying the book, the butterfly was not made from the same leather as the rest of the binding. It was, in fact, made of a piece of the author's own skin—the butterfly, a tattoo. The author chose to remain anonymous. The print run was one copy and, fortunately, the book never went back to press.

• • •

THE term "blurb," meaning a publisher's puff piece, was coined by Gelett Burgess in a speech at the 1907 American Booksellers Association dinner in New York City. He described his invention as a "sound like a publisher."

• • •

A medieval library showing each book chained to the bookcase.

THE dust jacket was originally born out of a need to protect a book's covers, given modern distribution techniques. The idea was a plain brown-paper wrapper. Using the jacket as an added way to promote what lay beneath did not come into vogue until after World War I. The idea was a pragmatic one. Extra jackets could be run off and used to replace those damaged in shipping.

* * *

DOUBLEDAY and Company once published a book titled, *The Sleeping Partner*, with different types of paper for each of its thirty-two-page signature. Publisher William Jovanovich remarked at the time, "This is, no doubt, a way to clear out one's inventory in the name of Art."

* * *

IT was Alfred A. Knopf Publishers who first came out with a book titled, *Coup D'Etat*, by Edward Luttwak, in two differently designed jackets. The thought was that booksellers could then promote the book with a two-tone display.

* * *

AUTHOR Alexander King had his publisher put two different jackets on his book—one inside the other. The inner jacket was appropriately subdued, while the visible jacket was a copy of one of his lusty paintings. The reader could decide how he wanted to display the book in his personal library.

IT is thought Grove Press was the first house to publish a book with three different jacket designs. The booksellers could order the jacket they liked best. This little device made the bookseller feel a part of the production process and so, the publishers of *Commander Amanda* hoped, would pay close attention to the book.

• • •

IN 1925, the *New York Times* reported that the practice of printing an author's portrait on the cover of his or her books had spread to France. Monsieur Regis Gignoux took a humorous but still dim view of this publishing innovation. He pointed out that henceforth the author would have to provide his publisher with a succession of photographs. "He will need a certain type for the first romance, full of life and high spirits. But after he has suffered his disillusions and begun to write in the current vein of despair of the whole human race he will need to display clothes much disordered and a face visibly harrowed with pessimism."

• • •

THE University of Chicago Press instituted a cost-saving idea of printing up a jacket with a four-color photograph of the campus on the front. The jacket flaps were blank and had no type on the front or back covers. For titles with small first printings, the name of the book, author biography, and description of the text would simply be overprinted on the generic jacket. Six titles were published in the 1960s using up the stock of the jackets, before this unique practice was discontinued.

THE following is taken from a review of John Keats's poetry that appeared in *Blackwood's* magazine in 1818:

> John Keats' friends, we understand, destined him to the career of medicine, and he was bound apprenticed to a worthy apothecary in town. . . . It is a better and wiser thing to be a starved apothecary than a starved poet, so back to the shops, Mr. John, back to plasters, pills and ointment boxes. But for heaven's sake, be a little more sparing of extenuatives and soporifics in your practice than you have been in your poetry.

• • •

THE impact of Sinclair Lewis's novel, *Main Street*, was far-reaching. Mark Schorer called it, "The most sensational event in twentieth century American publishing history." Two years after the book's publication, John Farrar wrote in *The Bookman,* describing the incremental popularity of the novel:

> Lewis's friends all bought the book, then the cognoscenti, then the literati, then the literate, a paltry thousand or so. Then the sleeping beast turned over, rubbed it eyes, and woke up. Fifty thousand. It howled in ecstasy of self-torture. One hundred thousand. His publishers estimated that it has beyond doubt reached two million readers. And people are still buying and reading it for the first time.

TRAVELING in Delhi, Mark Twain was roused one morning to find two monkeys that somehow had managed to get into his hotel room. He reported, "When I woke, one of them was before the glass brushing his hair and the other one had my notebooks, and was reading a page of humorous notes, and crying. I did not mind the one with the hairbrush, but the conduct of the other one hurt me; it hurts me still."

. . .

OF literary critics, Lord Byron wrote:

As soon
Seek roses in December—ice in June;
Hope constancy in wind, or corn in chaff;
Believe a woman or an epitaph,
Or any other thing that's false, before
You trust in critics.

Brendan Behan said of drama critics, "Critics are like eunuchs in a harem. They're there every night, they see it done every night, they see how it should be done every night, but they can't do it themselves."

. . .

ON May 17, 1928, the *Times Literary Supplement* received a letter from an annoyed author of a book they had critiqued. The author did not object to the review but to the assumed nature of his sex. Evelyn Waugh was not pleased at having been repeatedly addressed as "Miss Waugh" throughout the review.

REVIEWERS are not always as prophetic as the tone of their reviews might have the reader believe. The *North British Review,* for example, said of a new novel on the scene, "Here all the faults of *Jane Eyre* are magnified a thousand fold, and the only consolation which we have in reflecting upon it is that it will never be generally read." The book they dismissed so lightly was by the sister of the author of *Jane Eyre* and was titled, *Wuthering Heights.*

. . .

WHITNEY Balliett reviewed a novel for *The New Yorker* in 1961, saying, "[The author] wallows in his own laughter and finally drowns in it. What remains is a debris of sour jokes, stage anger, dirty words, synthetic looniness, and the sort of antic behavior that children fall into when they know they are losing our attention." The book was *Catch-22,* by Joseph Heller.

. . .

A REVIEW of Theodore Dreiser's *An American Tragedy* was published in the *Boston Evening Transcript* in 1925. The critic wrote:

> The commonplace of the story is not alleviated in the slightest degree by any glimmer of an imaginative insight on the part of the novelist. A skillful writer would be able to arouse an emotional reaction in the reader but at no moment does he leave him otherwise but cold and unresponsive. One feature of the novel stands out above all others—the figure of Clyde Griffiths. If the novel were great, he would be a great

character. As it is, he is certainly one of the most despicable creations of humanity that ever emerged from the novelist's brain. Last of all, it may be said without fear of contradiction that Mr. Dreiser is a fearsome manipulator of the English language. His style, if style it may be called, is offensively colloquial, commonplace and vulgar.

• • •

HOLLYWOOD and writers have always made uneasy bedfellows. Ernest Hemingway never quite got over the movie based on his book, *The Snows of Kilimanjaro*. He always referred to it as "The Snows of Zanuck" and gave his own best-performer award to the hyena.

• • •

VETERAN editor Patrick O'Connor once carried on a personal crusade to find an American publisher for a series of English novels that were favorites of his. He managed to slip the six "Lucia" novels, by E. F. Benson, onto the list at New American Library, but the books sold so poorly that NAL let the rights go. O'Connor had since gone over to Popular Library and, undaunted, he bought the paperback rights and started shopping for a hardcover publisher. After carefully wining and dining an editor at Thomas Y. Crowell, O'Connor was crushed to find the editor did not think the series had a prayer of getting through the editorial board at Crowell. In desperation, O'Connor said, "But what are you going to do when these books appear on Masterpiece Theater?" The exaggeration worked, and the books were published in hardcover by Crowell in one volume titled, *Make Way for Lucia.*

The book was a huge success, but to O'Connor's discomfort, reviews and articles about the book often mentioned that *Lucia* was to be featured on "Masterpiece Theater." One day, O'Connor's secretary announced a call for him; it was someone from "Masterpiece Theater" on the phone. "Well, Mr. O'Connor," the woman on the line said. "We've traced this lie to you." After letting the editor squirm a bit, she let O'Connor off the hook. "Now that these books have been brought to our attention, we're quite interested." The novel appeared in dramatic form on the program and was broadcast in 1986.

• • •

REBECCA West recalled her experiences as a Hollywood screenwriter from a formal distance and without great fondness:

> The largest sum I ever earned out of a single piece of work was from the sale of a story to a film corporation which in my youth I took down from the lips of another woman. Both she and I were paid large sums of money for the film rights. The film corporation used not a single line of dialogue that was in my record, and it changed the title and names of the characters. What they had paid me for was a mystery, and I made it the more mysterious by insisting that my name was removed from the screen credits. A gift from a fairy godmother is less acceptable when she turns out to be the village idiot.

ONE of the shrewdest negotiators on a film project must have been producer Gabriel Pascal. George Bernard Shaw, with whom he was corresponding regarding the purchase of the screenplay rights to one of the eminent playwright's works, asked for $8,000. Pascal countered with an offer of $4,000. As the transatlantic/transcontinental bargaining continued, Shaw protested that Pascal must not have understood the original demand. "What I asked for was $80,000, not eight." Pascal wired back, "Excuse error, I'll give you $40,000."

• • •

PAUL S. Nathan reported in his *Publishers Weekly* column:

> Well, it didn't work—MGM's attempt to get a screenplay out of *Brideshead Revisited* (Little, Brown) and now Evelyn Waugh, who was to have adapted his own book for pictures, has shaken the parched dust of Hollywood from his feet. There had been some doubt right along that Mr. Waugh could square his story, which had certain touchy religious angles, with the Motion Picture Production Code, but apparently the studio must have had reasonable grounds for hope before importing the novelist all the way from England.

This item appeared in the April 5, 1947, issue thirty-four years before the extraordinary success of the Granada-TV presentation on public broadcasting which propelled Waugh's novel onto the bestseller list in 1982.

S OME years ago, Random House issued a new edition of
The History of Henry Esmond in its Modern Library
series. Shortly after the novel was published, the editors
were startled to receive a letter from a well-known Hollywood agency addressed to the author, William Makepeace
Thackeray, Esq., who had breathed his last a century before.
The letter read: "We have read your recent book, The History
of Henry Esmond, and it possesses material adaptable for
motion pictures. We are recognized agents for writers at all
studios and as such would like to represent you in the sale of
both your own personal services and your literary products."
The letter continued,

> In the event that you have already made a commit-
> ment to some agent for the above book, we neverthe-
> less are impressed with your potential possibilities as a
> screen writer and would be interested in both your
> services and future stories. We would appreciate your
> advising us by return mail whether or not you are
> represented here in Hollywood; we would be happy to
> forward your copy of our agency agreement with writ-
> ers for your information and guidance.

Since publishers are always looking out for opportuni-
ties for their authors—be they alive or dead—Random
House wrote back the following:

> Thank you for your letter telling me that my recent
> book, The History of Henry Esmond, possesses material
> adaptable for motion pictures. This effort is a rather
> crude attempt, I fear, but I am now working on a new
> novel which I think will be a natural for pictures. I am

thinking of calling the new book, *Vanity Fair.* I will be interested in hearing what you think of the title.

The letter was signed, "Sincerely yours, William Makepeace Thackeray."

A few days later, another letter arrived from the agency saying,

Acknowledging receipt of your letter of December 28, in reply to your previous communication, we feel that the title which you are thinking of giving your new book, namely, *Vanity Fair,* is a good one. Perhaps you could also send us a manuscript at this time, or if not, a copy of the book, *The History of Henry Esmond.* We would like to submit this, if we are authorized to do so by you, to the studios for their consideration.

Alas, production has yet to be started on "Henry Esmond."

• • •

ON October 26, 1809, the *New York Evening Post* carried the following announcement, "Distressing—Left his lodgings some time since and has not since been heard of, a small, elderly gentleman, dressed in an old black coat and cocked hat, by the name of Knickerbocker." Then, two weeks later, an item appeared saying that a man fitting that description had been spotted on a stagecoach heading for Albany. Ten days later, the paper carried a news story that the landlord of the Columbian Hotel had found a handwritten manuscript he believed had been left by the mysterious Knickerbocker. Seth Handaside(!), the hotel manager, decided to sell the manuscript in order to settle the bill the elusive boarder had failed to pay. Months later, the book, a two-volume set, appeared in bookstores (selling for $3), bearing the title *The History of New York*, by Diedrich Knickerbocker. It was a huge success. The author of the book and of the elaborate hoax was Washington Irving, who wanted to create a unique publicity campaign for the book and have a little joke on the New York reader. The name Died/rich Knickerbocker was his private joke.

• • •

COUNT Leo Tolstoy became a devout Christian late in life and spent his final days divesting himself of all his earthly possessions and, lastly, his estates. He asked his wife to see to it that all his writings be put in the public domain— so they could be freely enjoyed by everyone. The Countess Tolstoy was irate and tried to find his will to destroy it. The Count discovered her one night, rifling through his papers, and left the house in a rage. He boarded a train and caught pneumonia. He died shortly thereafter.

• • •

THE original draft of T. S. Eliot's *The Waste Land* was titled "The Quinn Manuscript" and was made up of *The Waste Land* and nine "satellite" poems. Ezra Pound took the unwieldy manuscript in hand and edited it drastically down to 433 lines and, because of its newfound potency, Pound felt comfortable seeing what he had once called, "the longest poem in the Englisch langwidge" published.

IN the 1860s, when the owners of newly built bath houses on the shores of the San Francisco Bay wanted to ensure they would have customers, they planted terrifying stories of captured sharks in the California newspapers. To add a little realism, it was reported there had been several massive, man-chomping beasts caught in waters most frequented by swimmers. In fact, the sharks were reused to the point where they had to let some go because they were looking increasingly pathetic, and new ones were imported from down the coast. The author of the fake shark stories was Mark Twain.

• • •

THE winner of a competition sponsored by an English journal had written what was voted the most accurate parody of Graham Greene's writings. It was published in the journal. A week later, a letter from Greene himself was published. He congratulated the winner, John Smith, but wondered why Joe Doakes and William Jones had not been awarded some kind of honorable mention. After all, Greene wrote, all three were entries of Greene's unpublished novels submitted by the author himself.

• • •

THERE have been several hoaxes involving the submission of established "classics" to the major publishing houses and literary agencies with the author's name removed. The first two chapters and a synopsis of *War and Peace,* according to Norman Cousins, was mailed out to ten publishers in the 1950s by a friend of Cousins's. Only four publishers spotted the material for what it was, while the others returned it with a basic letter of rejection. Jerzy Kosinki's award-winning *Steps* and William Faulkner's *The Reivers* have also been multiply submitted and an alarming majority rejected.

. . .

IN his book, *Winesburg, Ohio*, Sherwood Anderson wrote, " 'They think it is easy to be a woman, to be loved, but I know better,' he declared. Again he turned to the child. 'I understand,' he cried, 'perhaps of all men I understand. . . . I know about her, although she has never crossed my path. . . . It is because of her defeats that she is to me the lovely one.' " Six years later, a poem by Theodore Dreiser was published in a literary magazine:

> *They think it is easy to be a woman—*
> *To love and be loved.*
> *But I know better.*
> *Again and again I tell you*
> *I know.*
> *I understand.*
> *Perhaps, of all men,*
> *I understand.*
> *I know about her because*
> *She has crossed my path . . .*
> *It is because of her defeats*
> *That she is to me*
> *The lovely one.*

The parallel phrasings, which give a whole new meaning to the poetic form known as free verse, were pointed out by Franklin P. Adams in the *New York World*, in 1926.

M RS. Sinclair Lewis charged Theodore Dreiser with plagiarism when their books about their impressions of Russia were published almost simultaneously, in 1928. Her series of articles had appeared in the *New York Evening Post* from February 2 through March 3, and Dreiser's had been published by the *New York World* between March 18 and March 28. Their books were published within two months of one another (Dreiser's being the later). Dreiser's successful defense was that the books would have to have great similarities because they both used the only source available to them when researching in Russia—the *Weekly News Bulletin*, a Soviet publication issued in Moscow by the press section of the Department for Cultural Relations with Foreign Countries.

• • •

D URING 1910 and 1911, Jack London bought twenty-seven plot outlines from the then unknown Sinclair Lewis for a total of $137.50. It is generally acknowledged that London used some of these outlines in some of his own work (a novelette, *The Abyssmal Brute*; an unfinished novel titled, *The Assassination Bureau*; and three short stories, "When All the World was Young," "Winged Blackmail," and "The Prodigal Father"). It is interesting to note that, even at the bargain rate of $6 apiece, London rejected some of the other plots Lewis had submitted, saying in a letter, "A number of them are O. Henry plots. O. Henry would have handled them and they'd have been great with his style of handling."

O. HENRY was the pseudonym chosen by William Sydney Porter. A bank cashier charged with embezzling, Porter had fled to South America. He later surrendered himself and spent five years (1898–1903) in the Ohio penitentiary. He was made the night watchman of the prison infirmary and passed the time by writing short stories. He took the name O. Henry from a prison guard and started submitting the stories to magazines. Upon his release, he established a wide, dedicated following. However, a former acquaintance started blackmailing him, threatening to tell his adoring public about his experiences as an inmate. To pay for the blackmailer's silence, O. Henry began making a nuisance of himself by stopping by his publisher, Doubleday, late in the day, asking for small advances on his advances.

When the publisher of *Hampton's*, a small literary journal, offered him $500 for an original short story, O. Henry asked for half of the money up front to pay off the blackmailer. The editor agreed, promising the second half upon his receipt of the completed short story. O. Henry submitted the first half and did not hear from *Hampton's* until the writer noticed the magazine had printed the first half of the story without paying for it. The magazine placed a small advertisement at the end of the unfinished piece—offering $250 if anyone could complete it.

• • •

EDGAR Allan Poe perpetuated a successful hoax in the *New York Sun* with an article he wrote in the April 13, 1844, edition of the paper. He described the arrival, near Charleston, South Carolina, of a group of English "aeronauts" who, as he told the story, had crossed the Atlantic in a dirigible in just seventy-five hours. Poe had cribbed most of his narrative from an account by Monck Mason of an actual balloon trip he and his companions had made from London to Germany in November 1836. Poe's realistically detailed fabrication fooled everyone.

· · ·

THE *Atlantic Monthly* published a series on "Lincoln the Lover" in 1928. The articles were based on a cache of recently discovered correspondences between Abraham Lincoln and Ann Rutledge, letters that neatly verified the legend that Lincoln and Rutledge had been sweethearts since their early twenties. The letters turned out to be the efforts of a San Diego columnist, Wilma Minor. Before the hoax was uncovered, Minor had taken in the editors of the illustrious magazine and several respected Lincoln scholars. Even Carl Sandburg was duped. He wrote to Ellery Sedgewick, the editor of *The Atlantic Monthly*, "These new letters seem entirely authentic—and preciously and wonderfully coordinated and chime with all else known of Lincoln." When Minor was found out, it was also discovered that her daughter had participated in the hoax. Her daughter justified the conspiracy by explaining the letters were based upon messages she had received from the spirits of Lincoln and Rutledge.

ONE of the most celebrated literary hoaxes in the past fifty years was Clifford Irving's 1971 "autobiography" of Howard Hughes. Irving, who had written a previous book, ironically titled *Fake*, a biography of art forger Elmyr de Hory, approached McGraw-Hill with a transcript of conversations he claimed he had taped with Hughes. Substantiating the transcripts were handwritten documents written by Hughes to Irving. The material was fascinating and credible, and the package sold for a $750,000 advance.

Life magazine, skeptical at first, bought serialization rights; the Book of the Month Club and Dell Publishers fell in line with high advances. All were convinced the material was authentic until the publication date was announced and the first shadow of doubt emerged. Then Hughes Company officials denounced the book as a fraud. Time-Life executives were concerned and sought the advice of a handwriting specialist. The expert was confident; *Life* and McGraw-Hill stood by the book. The next move was made by the reclusive millionaire. Hughes called a friend at Time-Life and denounced the book in the well-known three-hour conference call that was televised. Irving claimed it could not have been Hughes, but already the hoax was beginning to unravel.

The final piece of evidence against Irving was the discovery that a Swiss bank account in the name of H. R. Hughes had actually been opened by a "Helga Hughes," a bewigged accomplice who turned out to be Irving's wife, Edith. The book, which had earned millions before its scheduled publication date was, of course, never published, and Irving was sent to prison.

I N May 1983, the West German photoweekly *Stern* announced the astounding discovery of sixty-two volumes of Adolf Hitler's long-lost secret diaries. Hailed by *Stern* as "the journalistic scoop of the post–World War II period," the leatherbound diaries were said to have been recovered from a 1945 plane crash and were being offered for serialization at up to $3 million. Rupert Murdoch jumped in with a $400,000 offer, while *Newsweek, Paris Match,* and Italy's *Panorama* snapped up translation rights for their markets. As an international furor over authenticity continued, several expert historians were enlisted to give their opinions. Hugh Trevor-Roper initially declared the diaries to be real. He soon changed his mind, however, when the German government declared flatly that the diaries were faked. An international race was on to prove once and for all whether the diaries were Hitler's own—or a scam. *Stern* correspondent Gerd Heidemann, the "discoverer" of the diaries, was finally revealed as the main culprit in the hoax.

ADDRESSING a lecture hall filled with aspiring student writers at Columbia University, Sinclair Lewis was asked to talk about the writer's craft. He stood at the dais and addressed the young hopefuls: "How many of you here are really serious about being writers?" The writer watched as a sea of waving hands shot up. "Well, why the hell aren't you all home writing?" With that, Lewis returned to his seat.

. . .

THE earliest versions of the story of Cinderella have her wearing slippers of white squirrel fur ("vair" in old French). The story was rewritten by the French author, Charles Perrault, and in his version of *Cendrillon*, published in 1679 in a collection of fairy tales, he mistook the word "vair" for "verre" (glass), and the error has remained in use since.

. . .

ELIZABETH Foster married Isaac Goose in 1693. She wrote little rhymes and stories for her grandchildren, which were eventually published under the name Mother Goose.

WRITERS have always been at the ready to give advice to aspiring authors. William Styron joined William Faulkner in urging writers to read anything. James Michener refined that thought by suggesting reading the great books— as many as possible—before turning twenty- two. John O'Hara talked about setting up a file system and writing forward and backward from an established climax. Ernest Hemingway believed the writer should possess seriousness and an innate talent. William Faulkner preached "experience, observation and imagination," while Stendhal had but one rule: "to be clear." Henry James centered his writing philosophy on simply making his fiction "interesting." John Steinbeck and Gabriel Garcia Marquez shared a habit of directing their writing to a single reader—a friend, preferably—and writing just to them. Ford Madox Ford believed in the story "and then your story—and then your story." Somerset Maugham, however, came up with the only one true, hard, and immutable rule: "There are three rules for writing a novel. Unfortunately, no one knows what they are."

• • •

IN the spring of 1965, Edmund Updale, a seventeen-year-old student attending Dulwich College in England, wrote to six authors he admired, asking for advice on becoming a writer. All six replied.

P. G. Wodehouse wrote a two-page letter and suggested Updale consider apprenticing himself to a newspaper. "I have always thought that was the ideal way for a writer to begin, because of the experience a reporter gets." He also advised the young man to be patient: "My agent over here showed me the other day the 'card' for one of my early stories, and it was refused by twenty-six editors before finally landing." Wodehouse even offered to review "a few specimens" if Updale wanted an opinion of his own work. W. Somerset Maugham wrote from his villa in Cap Ferrat. His note suggested to write "as simply as you can—as though you were writing a letter to a friend."

Evelyn Waugh's handwritten note advised studying Latin, grammar, and vocabulary and reading everything from the sixteenth, seventeenth, nineteenth, and twentieth centuries. Nicholas Monsarrat wrote on stationery sporting a logo of the P & O Lines of Canberra, Australia. Monsarrat made a list of specific things, summing up with "Sit down at the typewriter or notebook and get to work." J. B. Priestley urged Updale to read "good authors critically" to see how they structured their fiction and to keep a journal. Compton Mackenzie wrote a less enthusiastic note than his colleagues, saying, "There is no advice that I or anybody else can give on how to become a famous writer. Every writer who ever lived has had to find that out for himself. Thank you very much for your congratulations and I hope that one day I shall be able to write and congratulate you."

* * *

EDNA St. Vincent Millay's middle name came from an odd source—a hospital. Before she was born, her uncle, Charles Buzzell, was found in the hold of a ship, having been knocked unconscious while unloading freight. He had been locked below decks for nine days—without food or water. When he was discovered, he was taken to St. Vincent's Hospital in New York City, where, against all odds, he recovered. His sister, grateful for the care her brother had received, named her newborn daughter in honor of the hospital.

Parenthetically, Dylan Thomas was taken to Saint Vincent's hospital when he collapsed at the White Horse Tavern in Greenwich Village and died there that night. James Charlton was also born there.

• • •

BROWSING in the British Museum, Jack Kerouac found a reference to the derivation of his family name, which, it turns out, he could trace to Brittany (his first name was actually Jean-Louis). The inscription on the coat of arms of the Kerouacs, ironically, was "Work, Love, Suffer."

• • •

EMILY Dickinson chose as a mentor Thomas Wentworth Higginson who, in 1862, had just published a piece in *The Atlantic Monthly* offering advice to unpublished writers. She wrote to the public figure and asked if he would consider reading some of her poems, which he agreed to do. She sent him dozens of poems in the years that followed, but he advised her they were all too offbeat for publication. Of the ten or so poems thought to have been published during her lifetime, all were printed anonymously.

It should be noted that Higginson, ever the astute literary critic, wrote of Walt Whitman, "It is no discredit to Walt Whitman that he wrote *Leaves of Grass*, only that he did not burn it afterwards."

WHEN the Book of the Month Club included a selection titled, *Seven Gothic Tales*, in its April 1934 catalogue, a little note accompanied the entry. "No clue is available as to the pseudonymic author"—Isak Dinesen.

Karen Blixen's nom de plume was taken from her maiden name and, no doubt, as a tribute to her lover, Denys Finch-Hatton.

• • •

NATHANIEL Hawthorne's *Rappacini's Daughter* was published with an enthusiastic preface both praising the story and explaining its subtleties. It had been written by Aubepine. Aubepine, in French, means "hawthorn"—he had written the preface himself.

• • •

IN 1799, the British ambassador gave a set of the third edition of the *Encyclopedia Britannica* to His Majesty Fath Ali, the Persian shah. The shah was so taken with the books that he had "The Most Formidable Lord and Master of the Encyclopedia Britannica," added to his title.

• • •

CHARACTERS can take on dimensions of a living, breathing, real person for their creators and for the readers as well—and often do. D. H. Lawrence, while complimenting elements of *Madame Bovary*, backhanded, "But we cannot help resenting the fact that the great tragic soul of Gustave Flaubert is, so to speak, given only the rather commonplace bodies of Emma and Charles Bovary." T. S. Eliot wrote of Mark Twain's all-American boy, "We come to see Huck . . . as one of the permanent symbolic figures of fiction; not unworthy to take his place with Ulysses, Faust, Don Quixote, Don Juan, Hamlet, and the other great discoveries that man has made about himself."

Emily Bronte's dark, brooding character frightened even her. "Whether it is right or advisable to create beings like Heathcliff, I do not know; I scarcely think it is. But this I know; the writer who possesses the creative gift owns something of which he is not always the master—something that, at times, strangely wills and works for itself."

• • •

Gertrude the Kangaroo evolving over the years. In addition to this marsupial logo for Pocket Books, Simon & Schuster has sported the wallaby, a smaller member of the kangaroo family. And for a brief two-month period in the 70's, the name of Washington Square Press was changed to Quokkas, a tiny relative of the kangaroo.

POCKET and Colophon are trademarks of Simon & Schuster, Inc.

IT was to his beloved Beatrice that Dante dedicated *The Divine Comedy.* He wrote of her as, "the first delight of my soul"—"the glorious lady of my mind." Ironically, the truth of the matter is that Dante and Beatrice saw each other only for three brief moments in their lifetimes. The first time, they were barely nine years old. She caught his eye for a second, and Dante later rhapsodized, "From that day forward, love quite governed my soul." They did not see each other again until nine years later when they passed each other on a street in Florence. She was escorted by two ladies and, once again, she probably did not notice him. They met only once after that for the briefest time. Beatrice married and died when she was thirty-five—completely unaware she was a partner in one of the greatest love stories in literature.

• • •

DORIS Lessing spoke of the elation accompanying the act of getting, as Guy de Maupassant said, "black on white" and the reality of what follows. She said,

> I remember my agreeable surprise that I had a quarter of it done, then a half, then it was finished. It was despatched to London publishers. This was before air mail was reintroduced after the war. Six weeks' train and boat-time to England, then the publishers kept it their usual inexcusable time, then six weeks' boat and train-time back. The train took five days from Cape Town to Salisbury. This was the most valuable lesson in acquiring patience, and that calculated obstinacy which I regard as any writer's most valuable asset.

JOHN D. MacDonald received the galleys of his novel from his publisher several months after the assassination of President John F. Kennedy in November 1963. The main character was named Dallas, but both MacDonald and his editor, Knox Burger, felt a name change would be in order. As MacDonald related, "at the following friday writer's lunch, I told my friends my problem. Nobody could come up with a useful name and then Mackinlay Kantor said, 'go check the list of air force bases. They have good names.' I did, and there was Travis Air Force Base in California." The character was renamed Travis McGee, and the novel, *The Deep Blue Goodbye,* became the first in a perennially successful series.

• • •

WHEN her husband's novel, *The Beautiful and Damned,* was published, Zelda Fitzgerald was asked if the heroine was modeled after her. "It seems to me," she replied, "that on one page I recognize a portion of an old diary of mine which disappeared shortly after my marriage, and also scraps of letters which sound to me vaguely familiar. In fact, Mr. Fitzgerald—I believe that is how he spells his name— seems to believe that plagiarism begins at home."

• • •

WINSTON Churchill's collected speeches were published in England in 1938 under the title, *Arms and the Covenant.* His American publisher felt that the American audience would not be drawn to that title and so asked Churchill if he had a choice for a different title. He wired back, "THE YEARS OF THE LOCUST," which was misread by the cable operator and came through as "lotus" instead of "locust." The editors confessed among themselves they did not understand Churchill's selection but would honor the intent. Because the lotus, according to Greek legend, was thought to induce sleep, the book was published here as *While England Slept* and was hugely successful. It is interesting to note that John F. Kennedy's Harvard senior thesis, published in 1940, was titled, *Why England Slept.*

• • •

DICK Grossman was an editor at Simon and Schuster in the 1950s and was working on a first novel titled, *A Candle at Midnight,* by Sloan Wilson. The title did not evoke a clear enough picture of the subject—the world of big business—and Grossman began looking for a better one. Over dinner with publisher Dick Simon, Wilson's wife referred to her husband's Time-Life associates as "all those men in grey flannel suits." Simon liked the phrase and mentally designed the jacket. He said, pointing to Grossman, "And I know where we can get a model—free." Grossman protested, saying he did not even own a grey flannel suit. Simon pulled out several large bills and instructed the editor to buy a suit, "in any color." The photo was eventually used on the cover of *The Man in the Grey Flannel Suit,* and the book was an immediate best-seller. Gregory Peck assumed Grossman's stance for the movie advertisements and Grossman and the photographer received $400 from Twentieth Century Fox for the rights to the pose. It was Gregory Peck—alas, not Grossman—who appeared on the paperback cover.

MICKEY Spillane, addressing a Mystery Writers of America convention, warned his fans not to look too closely for symbolic depth in his novels. Of his famous character, Spillane said, "Mike Hammer drinks beer, not cognac, because I can't spell cognac."

• • •

MILA 18, Leon Uris's best-selling novel, was scheduled for publication by Doubleday in the late 1950s. Then sales manager, Sam Vaughan, got a call from his colleague at Simon and Schuster, Dick Grossman, who informed his friend that they had a first novel coming out at the same time as Uris's and that it, too, had the number 18 in the title and would Doubleday change theirs. Vaughan argued that Doubleday's book was an eagerly awaited novel by a major author and suggested, in a friendly but firm tone, that if any changes were to be made, Simon and Schuster ought to be the one making them. Grossman and the author, in the end, acquiesced. And so, Joseph Heller's novel was finally published, as *Catch-22*. Grossman recalls the novel was years in the writing and had first been catalogued as *Catch-14*.

• • •

FOR one of its main selections in 1951, the Book of the Month Club chose *The Catcher in the Rye*. Unsure of the novel's title, the editorial staff asked the author if he would consider another one. J. D. Salinger wrote back, "Holden Caulfield wouldn't like that," and so the matter was dropped.

ROBERT Penn Warren said he always remembered every detail of the time and place when inspiration hit. He said:

> For instance, *World Enough and Time*. Katherine Anne Porter and I were both in the Library of Congress as fellows. We were in the same pew, had offices next to each other. She came in one day with an old pamphlet, the trial of Beauchamp for killing Colonel Sharp. She said, "Well, Red, you better read this." There it was. I read it in five minutes. But I was six years making the book. Any book I write starts with a flash, but takes a long time to shape up.

• • •

THE Baroness Orczy says she was inspired to write *The Scarlet Pimpernel* while standing on the platform of the London subway stop, Temple Station. "Now of all the dull, prosey places in the world, can you beat an underground railway station? It was foggy, too, and smelly and cold. But I give you my word that as I was sitting there I saw—yes, I saw—Sir Percy Blakeney, just as you know him now."

• • •

ROBERT Louis Stevenson was thrashing about in his bed one night, greatly alarming his wife. She woke him up, infuriating Stevenson, who yelled, "I was dreaming a fine bogey tale!" The nightmare from which he had been unwillingly extracted was the premise for the story of *Dr. Jekyll and Mr. Hyde*.

A 1917 edition of *Publishers Weekly* carried a "letter" from Dr. Watson in which he explained where his famous colleague had been hiding himself.

> The friends of Mr. Sherlock Holmes will be glad to learn that he is still alive and well, though somewhat crippled by occasional attacks of rheumatism. He has, for many years, lived in a small farm upon the Downs, five miles from Eastbourne, where his time is divided between philosophy and agriculture. During this period of rest he has refused the most princely offers to take up various cases, having determined that his retirement was a permanent one. The approach of the German war caused him, however, to lay his remarkable combination of intellectual and practical activity at the disposal of the government, with historical results which are recounted in *His Last Bow*. Several previous experiences which have lain long in my portfolio have been added to *His Last Bow* so as to complete this volume.

Sir Arthur Conan Doyle's final collection of the master sleuth was published that year by George H. Doran Company, in the United States.

• • •

ACCORDING to Herbert Giles's *History of Chinese Literature*, in 13 B.C., a politician named Li Ssu took drastic measures to encourage new writers. He ordered all existing books burned so that literature could start afresh. Books on agriculture, medicine, and divination were exempted.

FRANK Doubleday decided to visit his good friend Rudyard Kipling at the writer's home in Sussex. He took a train and then decided to walk from the station to surprise Kipling. As the publisher neared Kipling's house, he noticed smoke coming from the chimney, which he thought odd considering it was a warm summer day. Concerned that perhaps the flue was on fire, Doubleday entered through the open front door and hurried to the study, where he found Kipling stoking a blazing fire with page after page of hand-written manuscript—a publisher's nightmare. "What are you doing?" Doubleday asked, appalled. "Well," Kipling answered, "I was looking over old papers and I got thinking. No one's going to make a monkey out of me after I die."

• • •

THOMAS Carlyle had to rewrite the first volume of his *History of the French Revolution* after John Stuart Mill had borrowed it to read, and his maid, mistaking it for trash, burned it. Carlyle later wrote he "had not only forgotten the structure of it, but the spirit it was written in was past."

• • •

THE husband of the typist who had been working on transcribing James Joyce's *Ulysses* manuscript, took a look and found the handwriting impossible to read. He assumed it was useless scrap, and so a chunk of Joyce's masterwork was lost to fire. Malcolm Lowry and Joseph Conrad lost entire manuscripts to fires in their homes. Blake wrote, "When commanded by spirits, and the moment I have written I see the words fly about the room in all directions. . . . My manuscripts are of no further use. I have been tempted to burn my manuscripts but my wife won't let me."

While writing his sequel to *Tom Sawyer*, Mark Twain wrote to his editor, "I like it only tolerably well, as far as I have gone, and may possibly pigeonhole or burn the manuscript when it is done." He kept it and titled it, *The Adventures of Huckleberry Finn*.

• • •

WHILE imprisoned for twelve years, Sir Walter Raleigh spent his time writing *The History of the World*. The first volume was published in 1614. His publisher, Walter Burre, would visit him in his cell. When Raleigh asked about the sales, Burre had to confess the book had thus far sold very slowly—so slowly, Burre added, it had all but ruined his business. Raleigh then took the second volume and final volume and said, "Ah, my friend, hath the first part undone thee, the second volume shall undo no more; this ungrateful world is unworthy of it." With that, he tossed it into the fireplace and watched sadly as the fire destroyed the pages. After Raleigh's death, the surviving first volume sold thousands of copies, making Burre a wealthy man.

• • •

THE first printing of John Steinbeck's, *The Wayward Bus*, was demolished when the truck carrying the books from the bindery crashed in flames. The truck had been hit by a "wayward" bus that had been traveling down the wrong side of the road.

ERICH Maria Remarque defined the differences between the typical American, French, and Russian novels. He defined the American novel as, "A story in which two people want each other from the beginning but don't get each other until the end of the book." The French novel was, "A story in which two people get together right at the beginning but from then until the end of the book they don't want each other any more." And, finally, the Russian novel was, "A story in which the two people don't want each other or get each other—and for 800 pages brood about it."

• • •

KEN McCormick, the former editor-in-chief of Doubleday and Company, recalls the time his secretary came in with the news that a manuscript on submission had fallen into the wastepaper basket and been thrown out. McCormick wrote the author asking for a carbon copy. The author replied that his masterpiece was the only copy and that he planned to sue the publishing company for snuffing out his literary brilliance. Doubleday's insurance company suggested an equitable settlement of some kind so McCormick wrote to his colleagues asking if they had read the manuscript and cared to venture on opinion as to its worth. Several editors wrote back saying they had rejected the work as "junk," while others wrote saying that, until the week before, they had that very manuscript on submission, but the author had called demanding it be returned. When confronted with the fact there existed many more copies of his priceless work than was originally thought, the author accepted a token settlement, and the matter was dropped.

WHEN he discovered that his dog had shredded his autographed copy of one of Ogden Nash's books, radio director Tom Carlson searched for a replacement for the much-loved volume that had long since gone out of print. He finally found a copy and mailed it to Nash to be autographed. In his letter to the poet, Carlson explained what had happened to his first copy. Nash returned the book with the following dedication: "To Tom Carlson, or his dog—depending on whose taste it best suits."

• • •

JOHN Steinbeck's Irish setter puppy, Toby, chewed up the only draft of the first half of *Of Mice and Men*. "Two months of work to do over again," Steinbeck wrote. "I was pretty mad at the time but the poor little fellow may have been acting critically." When the early reviews of the work were less than enthusiastic, Steinbeck remarked, "I'm not sure Toby didn't know what he was doing when he ate the first draft."

Sir Isaac Newton's dog destroyed a manuscript containing years of calculations and writings, to which Newton simply said, "Ah, poor Fidele, what mischief hast thou done."

THE celebrated writer Kay Boyle has had the nightmare of disappearing manuscripts occur twice in her career. The initial time was in the 1920s when she was living in Paris and a friend offered to send her first novel to a publisher in Chicago. Not having the money to make a copy, she turned the manuscript over and it, alas, disappeared forever.

The second unfortunate occurrence came in 1965, when, after two years of hard work, Boyle had completed half of her *Modern History of Germany*. Remembering the incident in Paris, she drove down from Cambridge with three copies of the manuscript, one to leave with her editor Ken McCormick and the second to take back with her to Radcliffe. The third copy was for a daughter living on Twenty-first Street with whom she was staying for the night. Parking in front of the building, Boyle left her luggage and manuscript locked in the car and went up to join the happy family reunion. Finally, excusing herself after dinner, she went downstairs only to find the car broken into and everything gone. A distraught Boyle returned to Cambridge to face the task of reconstructing the missing manuscript pages.

Meanwhile, the *Herald Tribune* ran a sympathetic story about the loss, and Mike Watkins, Boyle's literary agent, offered a reward with no questions asked for the manuscripts return. But to no avail. It was three weeks before a man telephoned Watkins and told him he had found three copies of the manuscript wrapped in brown paper in his garbage can. He would return the package, but not to the agent's office where, he said, the police might be. Finally, it was decided that they would meet in Grand Central Station at exactly twelve noon, where the man would leave the package in the last phone booth and step aside. Mike would then inspect the package, and if it was the right one, would slip a $50 bill under the phone book.

The drama was acted out as planned, and that afternoon Mike Watkins sent Kay Boyle a much-welcomed one-word telegram: "GOTEM."

• • •

WALT Whitman joyfully credited Ralph Waldo Emerson with getting *Leaves of Grass* noticed and accepted by the press and by the public. "I was simmering, simmering," wrote Whitman. "Emerson brought me to a boil." Emerson had written a glowing letter to Whitman that, at the urging of Charles Dana (editor of the *New York Sun*), Whitman added to the second, expanded edition of *Leaves of Grass*, which appeared in 1856. In part, the letter said:

> I greet you at the beginning of a great career, which must yet have had a long foreground somewhere, for such a start. I rubbed my eyes a little to see if this sunbeam were no illusion: but the solid sense of the book is a sober certainty. It has the best merits, namely of fortifying and engaging.

The public endorsement by this deeply respected, renowned philosopher, helped the book, considered too racy by the general public heretofore, to sell out each printing.

ALTHOUGH lost or destroyed manuscripts were more common before the advent of the photocopying machine and computer disks, mishaps still occur. Facing a deadline, a San Francisco writer loaded his word processor into the trunk of his car and headed to the Napa Valley to work undisturbed. It was raining heavily and the driving was slow. The writer pulled into a restaurant for dinner to wait out the storm. While he was eating, his car was struck by lightning, and every disk was erased.

· · ·

DURING these times of publishing conglomerates, one story making the rounds was that Norton Simon, the former publisher of *The Saturday Review,* was interested in acquiring a trade publishing company from Gulf & Western. Simon & Schuster was the rumored target, as was the old-line house of W. W. Norton. Had the deal gone through, the new imprint could have been, W. W. Norton Norton Simon Simon & Schuster.

· · ·

THE first encyclopedia was put together by three Scots: Colin Macfarquhar, a printer; William Smellie, a writer and scholar; and Andrew Bell, an engraver (mostly of dog collars). They printed their sourcebook, a pamphlet at a time, between 1768 and 1771. The definitions and explanations of all the various entries reflected their times. A type of disease afflicting horses, for example, was awarded some thirty-nine pages, while the entry for "woman" was, simply, "the female of man."

THE first "Portable" series was designed by Alexander Woollcott. Anthologies of popular American poetry and prose and literary classics were organized and selected for servicemen during World War II. They were successful because soldiers in the trenches could read a complete work in the short periods afforded them. The first ten editions of the Portable series included Shakespeare, the World Bible, and Dorothy Parker, and only those three have remained continually in print, selling consistently since the inception of the series.

• • •

IN 1934, Professor Dumas Malone became the director of Harvard University Press. He undertook a project he called "Scholarly-plus"—a gradual popularization of the list. Criticism was inevitable, and the director of Yale University Press made a particularly pointed comment when he noted that the so-called Scholarly-plus program included a mussel cookbook.

• • •

THE term "free lance" dates back to the Crusades of the twelfth century. Warrior knights allied themselves with a landed lord in exchange for property, salary, and the Middle Ages equivalent of a letter sweater—a coat of arms. However, they occasionally fell out of favor (perhaps by pushing their luck with one of their liege's daughters) or their sponsor died. Then, landless and unaffiliated, they could earn a living by offering themselves as mercenaries—a lance for hire.

IN Arnold Bennett's the *Old Wives' Tale*, there is a scene describing a public execution. Frank Harris, reviewing the book, said it was obvious the author had never witnessed such a thing and that his imagination had distorted the picture. Harris then proceeded to describe what an execution was actually like, and his account was so terrifyingly realistic, Bennett wrote him, "If your description only had appeared before mine, I assuredly would have utilized it. Of course you have discovered my secret. I never have witnessed an execution." Frank Harris wrote back, "Neither have I."

•   •   •

A HOUSEPAINTER in his youth, Brendan Behan was asked by the owner of a Parisian cafe to draw a sign in the window to entice English-speaking tourists. Behan complied with the following:

> Come in, you Anglo-Saxon swine
> And drink of my Algerian wine.
> 'Twill turn your eyeballs black and blue,
> And damn well good enough for you.

Behan accepted payment for his creation and took his leave before the sign could be translated.

•   •   •

SOME writers harbored somewhat hidden talents. James Joyce won a bronze medal for singing in a Dublin festival (and subsequently threw the award into a river). Lord Byron was a formidable swimmer. He clocked himself as he swam the unpredictable waters of the Hellespont, managing it in seventy minutes. He later wrote to a friend, "This morning I swam from Sestos to Abydos. The immediate distance is not above a mile, but the current renders it hazardous;—so much so that I doubt whether Leander's conjugal affection must have been a little chilled in his passage to paradise."

• • •

EUGENE O'Neill honed his skills as a reporter for the *London Telegraph*. New to the job and eager to do well, he handed in a story that came back with the following note from his editor:

> This is a lovely story, but would you mind finding out the name of the gentleman who carved the lady and whether the dame is his wife or daughter or who? And phone the hospital for a hint as to whether she is dead or discharged or what? Then put the facts into a hundred and fifty words and send this literary batik to the picture framers.

• • •

EZRA Pound was an accomplished fencer and once challenged British poet and critic Lascelles Abercrombie to a duel over a disagreement. Abercrombie pointed out that, as the challenged party, he had the choice of weapons and suggested, "that we bombard each other with unsold copies of our own books." Pound, embarrassed at how much more "ammunition" he had, withdrew the challenge.

OMAR Khayyam, the author of the *Rubaiyat*, was a mathematician who pioneered the use of graphics to represent algebraic functions.

• • •

WILLIAM Carlos Williams said, "I don't play golf, am not a joiner, I vote Democratic, read as much as my eyes will stand, and work at my trade day in and day out. When I can find nothing better to do, I write." William Carlos Williams practiced medicine in Rutherford, New Jersey, specializing in children's diseases.

• • •

NINON de Lenclos, a renowned French courtesan, lay on her deathbed and, knowing the end was near, called in her lawyer, Arouet. She asked that a small sum be put aside for a simple funeral and that 1,000 francs be left to the lawyer's son, who was studying with the Jesuits, for his books. The young man's name was Francois-Marie Arouet, who later took the pseudonym of Voltaire.

• • •

CHARGED with stealing a deer from the estates of Sir Thomas Lucy of Charlecote, Stratford-upon-Avon, the thief retaliated with a ballad he sang publicly. The local magistrate found the song so "bitter," he prosecuted the author, who was obliged to leave the area for some time and live in London. The deer-stealer was William Shakespeare.

IN 1571, Miguel de Cervantes fought in the sea battle of Lepanto and was shot three times, once through his left hand, "for the greater glory of the right," he claimed. He was taken prisoner by the Barbary corsairs and sold into slavery in Algiers. He was ransomed by the priests of the Order of Mercy in 1580 and returned home to finish the story he had begun in prison, *Don Quixote*.

• • •

SOME authors started to sparkle early. Nathaniel Hawthorne wrote to his mother from school, "I do not want to be a doctor and live by men's diseases, nor a minister to live by their sins, nor a lawyer and live by their quarrels. So I don't see there is anything left for me but to be an author."

• • •

EDITH Wharton, at eleven, wrote the opening lines to her first "novel." " 'Oh, how do you do Mrs. Brown?' said Mrs. Tompkins. 'If only I had known you were going to call, I should have tidied up the drawing room.' " Her mother reviewed the writing sample and told her daughter, "Drawing rooms are always tidy."

A S a seventeen-year-old schoolboy, Charles Baudelaire wrote to his mother, Caroline Aupick:

> I'm very cross with myself; it looks as if I'm not going to have any success; I admit my self-esteem is deeply affronted. . . . You'll tell me: read a book. Well, goodness me, I've done nothing but read since I last saw you. . . . I'm absolutely fed up with literature: I can truly say that ever since I've been able to read I've not yet found a book that entirely pleased me, that I could like from the first page to the last page and so I don't read anymore. I'm stuffed with literature.

• • •

A MIABLY discussing the validity of ghosts, Lord Byron and Percy Bysshe Shelley decided to try their poetic skills at writing the perfect horror story. While nothing came of their efforts, Shelley's young wife, Mary Wollstonecraft, overheard the challenge and went about telling her own. It began, "It was on a dreary night of November that I beheld the Accomplishment of my toils." Her work was published in 1818, when she was twenty-one, and was titled *Frankenstein*.

• • •

A "LITERARY sensation" of 1919 was the publication in the United States of *The Young Visitors; or Mr. Salteena's Plan*. It was written by a British girl, Daisy Ashford, when she was nine years old. Daisy was thirty when the book was actually published. The publication had resulted when a group of Daisy's friends showed it to Sir James Barrie, who consented to write an introduction. And therein lay the controversy. Could a child have written this, or was it truly the efforts of Barrie, the creator of Peter Pan? Due in part to the argument over authorship, the book was an international best-seller for three years, making Daisy the youngest author to ever enjoy such success.

Another small novel written by an American girl at about the same time, had to wait even longer to become a best-seller—fifty-eight years, to be exact. Eleven-year-old Virginia Cary Hudson wrote the delightful *O Ye Jigs and Julips* and in 1962, the fifty-page book was published by Macmillan to rave reviews. The book became an instant best-seller and stayed on the list for two years. Both books are still in print.

• • •

EDGAR Allan Poe was expelled from West Point in 1831 for "gross neglect of duty." The explanation for his dismissal had to do with his following, to the letter, an order to appear on parade grounds in parade dress, which, according to the West Point rule book, consisted of "white belt and gloves." Poe reportedly arrived with his rifle, dressed in his belt and gloves—and nothing else.

• • •

TRAVELING along the Italian Riviera, Lord Bulwer-Lytton, done up in an embarrassingly elaborate outfit, acknowledged the stares of passersby. Lady Lytton, amused at his vanity, suggested it was not admiration but "that ridiculous dress" that caught people's eyes. Lytton responded, "You think that people stare at my dress and not at me? I will give you the most absolute and convincing proof that your theory has no foundation." Keeping on only his hat and boots, Lord Lytton removed every other article of clothing and rode in his open carriage for ten miles to prove his point.

Lord Tennyson was also keen on bizarre costumes and, especially during his later years, enjoyed keeping his hair at shoulder-length and wearing a monstrous black sombrero. He completed the "look" with a Byronic shirt and tie and a cloak worn over his shoulder like a musketeer. He once complained to a dinner companion that it was one of the biggest drawbacks of being a celebrity—that people stared and could sometimes not resist following him. The woman's young daughter offered, "Perhaps, sir, if you cut your hair and dressed like other people, they wouldn't stare so much." Tennyson was unamused.

This proves George Bernard Shaw's observation, "My main reason for adopting literature as a profession was that, as the author is never seen by his clients, he need not dress respectably."

• • •

WRITING to his daughter, F. Scott Fitzgerald commented on a book by Tom Wolfe, "However, the book doesn't commit the cardinal sin; it doesn't fail to live." Fitzgerald must have liked that line, too, because twenty years before, Edmund Wilson had written of a new novel, "I have said that [the novel] commits almost every sin that a novel can possibly commit; but it does not commit the unpardonable sin; it does not fail to live." The novel was *This Side of Paradise*, by F. Scott Fitzgerald.

N OT all writers were sustained by deeply rooted faith in their work. For example, in June 1851, Herman Melville wrote to Nathaniel Hawthorne:

> In a week or so, I go to New York, to bury myself in a third-story room, and work and slave on my "whale" while it is driving through the press. That is the only way I can finish it now—I am so pulled hither and thither by circumstances. The calm, the coolness, the silent grass-growing mood in which a man ought to always compose,—that, I fear, can seldom be mine. Dollars damn me; and the malicious Devil is forever grinning in upon me, holding the door ajar. . . . What I feel most moved to write, that is banned,—it will not pay. So the product is a final hash, and all my books are botches.

George Orwell was similarly wracked by self-doubt. In an essay titled "Why I Write," Orwell complained, "I have not written a novel for seven years, but I hope to write another fairly soon. It is bound to be another failure, every book is a failure, but I do know with some clarity what kind of book I want to write." Two years later, 1984 was published. Thirty-five years later it was once again a bestseller—in its title year.

• • •

F. SCOTT Fitzgerald had been supremely confident his first novel, *This Side of Paradise,* would be published and would sell well. He was not as cocky with *Tender Is the Night.* He wrote to his editor, Max Perkins, "The novel will certainly have *succés d'estime* but it may be slow in coming—

alas, I may again have written a novel for novelists with little chance of its lining anybody's pockets with gold." Fitzgerald had also predicted a short life for *The Great Gatsby* when, writing again to Max Perkins, he allowed, "If the book fails commercially it will be from one of two reasons or both. First, the title is only fair, rather than good. Second and most important, the book contains no important woman character, and women control the fiction market at present. I don't think the unhappy end matters particularly."

• • •

EVERY writer has a schedule for writing—even if it is to ignore schedules and create only when the Muse is sitting cross-legged on the typewriter, like a torch singer on a piano. Some writers require a charm or talisman, a time of day, a special kind of light, particular pencils, or, simply, a room of their own.

Ernest Hemingway got himself in the mood by sharpening dozens of pencils and then, like Virginia Woolf and Lewis Carroll, wrote standing up. Contrarily, Truman Capote, Mark Twain, and Robert Louis Stevenson wrote lying down.

Edmond Rostand, the author of *Cyrano de Bergerac*, claimed he was reduced to writing in his bathtub because his social calendar kept him from his work. Raymond Carver took to his car to avoid interruptions. Willa Cather insisted on reading a passage from the Bible before sitting down to write, while W. Somerset Maugham reread *Candide*, "so that I may have in the back of my mind the touch-stone of that lucidity, grace and wit."

Rudyard Kipling had to have dark inks for his pen. John Steinbeck preferred round pencils (" a hexagonal pencil cuts my fingers after a long day") that were sent to him by his editor. Vladimir Nabokov was not wedded to any particular schedule but did require lined bristol cards and "well sharpened, not too hard, pencils capped with erasers." Thomas Wolfe enjoyed a long walk before parking himself to write.

Budd Shulberg joked about the writer's uncanny ability to avoid work. His habit was, "First I clean the typewriter. Then I go through my shelves and return all borrowed books. Then I play with my three children. Then, if it's warm, I go for a swim. Then I find some friends to have a drink with. By then, it's time to clean the typewriter again."

• • •

GEORGES Simenon said he needed only a beginning, and once he had settled on it, he was compelled to begin writing the novel immediately. He explained his habit of keeping little notes beforehand, "I put only the names of the characters, their ages, their families. I know nothing whatever about the events which will occur later. Otherwise it would not be interesting to me." Once Simenon had started writing he would complete a chapter a day until the novel was finished. "Because it is a strain, I have to keep pace with the novel. If, for example, I am ill for 48 hours I have to throw away the previous chapters. And I never return to that novel. . . . I feel what he [his character] feels . . . and it's almost unbearable after five or six days. That is one of the reasons why my novels are so short; after eleven days I can't—it's impossible." Simenon has not written a novel since the death of his daughter.

L EO Tolstoy advocated an early start and clean living:

> I always write in the morning. I was pleased to hear lately that Rousseau too, after he got up in the morning, went for a short walk and sat down to work. . . . Many writers work at night. Dostoyevsky always wrote at night. In a writer there must always be two people—the writer and the critic. And, if one works at night, with a cigarette in one's mouth, although the work of creation goes on briskly, the critic is for the most part in abeyance, and this is very dangerous.

Contrarily, John O'Hara preferred working from midnight until dawn to avoid the quotidian interruptions that disturbed the creative flow. James Russell Lowell, however, offered some superb advice to Charles Eliot. "If one waits for the right time to come before writing, the right time never comes."

Anthony Trollope set himself a schedule so rigorous, he tempered it by suggesting, "All those who have lived as literary men—working daily as literary labourers,—will agree with me that three hours a day will produce as much as a man ought to write." Trollope then divided those three hours into fifteen-minute intervals in which he demanded 250 words of himself.

• • •

W ILLIAM F. Buckley typically writes his popular novels in 150 hours. He estimated that if Anthony Trollope had a word processor, "He'd have written, in three and one-half hours at my typing speed, not 3,500 words [Trollope's daily output] but 16,800 words per day."

WILLIAM Dean Howells urged Mark Twain to complete *The Adventures of Tom Sawyer*. Twain wrote to Howells outlining his frenzied schedule:

> I have written eight or nine hundred manuscript pages in such a brief space of time that I musn't name the number of days; I shouldn't believe it myself, and of course couldn't expect you to. I used to restrict myself to four or five hours a day and five days in the week, but this time I have wrought from breakfast till 5:15 P.M. six days a week, and once or twice I smouched a Sunday when the boss wasn't looking.

• • •

SIR Walter Scott had achieved wealth, fame (he was immensely popular throughout Europe and was widely translated), and a baronetcy. He said he lived "in a mist about money" and gave no thought to spending his earnings on his family and friends. However, at fifty-five, in ill health and contemplating retirement, Scott was informed he was penniless—in fact, in debt for over 130,000 pounds. He returned to his writing desk, saying, "I will involve no friend, either rich or poor . . . my own right hand shall do it." He wrote the novel *Woodstock* in three months and sold it for 8,228 pounds. He followed this with his "pot-boiler" titled, *Life of Napoleon*, which earned him 18,000 pounds, and a series of short stories and essays. In two years, he had managed to earn 40,000 pounds (approximately one half of which represented royalties from his earlier works). His creditors were delighted and so moved by his herculean efforts that they met and passed the following resolution:

That Sir Walter Scott be requested to accept of his furniture, plates, linens, paintings, library, and curiosities of every description, as the best means the creditors have of expressing their very high sense of his most honorable conduct, and in grateful acknowledgement for the unparalleled and most successful exertions he has made and continues to make for them.

• • •

LEO Toltsoy said, "If you ask someone, 'Can you play the violin?' and he says, 'I don't know, I've not tried, perhaps I can,' you laugh at him. Whereas about writing, people always say: 'I don't know, I have not tried,' as though one had only to try and one would become a writer."

• • •

ADDRESSING an American Booksellers Association convention, F. Scott Fitzgerald explained his writing speed with respect to his novel, *Tender Is the Night.* "In fact to write it, it took three months; to conceive it—three minutes; to collect the data in it—all my life."

L ORD Byron had an extremely prolific period between 1812 and 1816. He wrote *The Corsair* in ten days while pacing Albemarle Street at night. The work sold fourteen thousand copies the day it was published in 1814. He wrote *The Bridge of Abydos* in four days. Of his remarkable output and steady reception, Byron said, "This I take to be a humiliating confession, as it proves my want of judgment in publishing, and the public in reading things which cannot have stamina or permanence." Matthew Arnold responded, "The producer of such poems could not but publish them, and the public could not but read them. Nor could Byron have produced his work in any other fashion. . . . He wrote, as he truly tells us, to relieve himself, and he went on writing because he found the relief indispensable."

• • •

W HEN Alfred Hitchcock telephoned Georges Simenon, he was told he was working (on his 158th novel). Madame Simenon told the director that, because her husband was writing, she would rather not disturb him. Knowing of Simenon's speed, Hitchcock joked, "Let him finish his book; I'll hang on."

• • •

W HILE some writers describe the process as all agony, gloom, and painful extraction, others report the opposite experience when writing. Eudora Welty said, "Really, it just delights me to write. Sometimes I think about P. G. Wodehouse, who was said to laugh as he wrote. Well, sometimes I do too." E. M. Forster proclaimed, "I think I am different from other writers; they profess much more worry (I don't know if it's genuine). I have always found writing pleasant, and don't understand what people mean by 'throes of creation.' " Washington Irving confided, "I have never found, in anything outside of the four walls of my study, an enjoyment equal to sitting at my writing-desk with a clean page, a new theme, and a mind awake."

• • •

DANIEL Defoe is best remembered for his novel, *The Adventures of Robinson Crusoe*. However, Defoe was the author of over 250 books and pamphlets and predicted such institutions as a government agency for sailors, credit banks for farmers, and a British poor relief. Defoe had spent time in Newgate Prison as a child because of debts incurred by his parents.

• • •

THE most prolific author of this century, is Kathleen Lindsay, who has written 904 novels under six pen names. John Creasey and Georges Simenon have each written over 500 books.

• • •

ERLE Stanley Gardner is credited by the *Guinness Book of World Records* as being the fastest author of this century. It was his habit to tape 3-by-5-inch index cards around his study. Each index card explained where and when certain key incidents would occur in each detective novel. He then dictated to a crew of secretaries some ten thousand words a day, on up to seven different novels at a time.

Why is it more interesting to spend an evening with this book than with a beautiful woman?

A DELL BOOK
A COMPARISON TEST CHART
BOOK ⬇   WOMAN ⬇

BOOK			WOMAN
49%		TEXTURE	100%
100%		AVAILABILITY	2-100% (depending on competition)
60,000		NUMBER OF WORDS	11
97%		LAUGHTER PRODUCTION	3% average
0		MISERABILITY (capacity to make you feel terrible)	73%
80%		INSOMNIABILITY (ability to keep you up all night, one way or another)	79%
100%		OVERCOATABILITY (ease of placing in overcoat pocket)	11%
25¢		COST	$45 for dinner (wine and cabs not included)

A 1951 ad for a Dell mystery.

ISAAC Asimov recalls sitting in front of his new word processor to begin work on his 300th-odd book. He confidently switched the machine on. Nothing happened—no hum, no pop, no friendly greeting on the screen. After tinkering with the machine as much as he dared, he called the local Radio Shack. The clerk asked him if he had a service contract and Asimov explained he was a spokesman for the Tandy Corporation and had been given the machine. The clerk was not impressed and informed the author he would have to purchase a service contract before a repairman could be sent out. Asimov raced down to the shop to fill out the forms (and hand over a check for $1,402) and then had to wait for the approval from the Texas headquarters. Returning home to await the repairman, Asimov watched the hours slide by. Finally, the man showed up. He inspected the machine and then strolled over to the wall switch and flicked it on. The machine hummed warmly, and the repairman took his leave.

• • •

IN this age of computer typesetting and photoprinting, it is easy to forget that just a few years ago books were printed from brass and copper plates. Finely illustrated children's books, for example, required massive marble plates and an acid etching process. The D'Aulaires, a husband-and-wife team who have written and illustrated dozens of children's books, used this process. Hand drawings were laboriously transferred onto the marble slabs, which they could never get themselves to throw out. The plates accumulated in their apartment until the inevitable happened—the floor began to cave in under the weight.

HAROLD Brodkey's novel, *A Party of Animals*, gives new meaning to the term "long-awaited." The original contract for the book was signed in 1960 with Farrar, Straus and Giroux. Although some excerpts appeared in several magazines, the three thousand-page manuscript was not delivered to the publisher until 1976. Based on their reading of the published excerpts, the Book of the Month Club chose it as an alternate selection, assuming publication was a year or so away. But three years later, despite its annual appearance in their catalogues, the book remained unpublished. In 1979, it was reported that Brodkey had withdrawn the manuscript from Farrar, Straus and Giroux and had walked it over to Alfred A. Knopf. It was rumored Knopf paid Brodkey more than Roger Straus for a manuscript Straus referred to as "a sort of life in progress." To date, the novel remains unpublished.

• • •

SAMUEL Taylor Coleridge became an opium addict in his thirties and would chatter nonstop for hours. An audience was not essential. Charles Lamb claimed he once encountered Coleridge in a secluded garden of a mutual friend. Coleridge took Lamb by his lapel button and started off, eyes closed, on a long-winded soliloquy. Lamb cut off the button and left. When he happened by the garden five hours later, Lamb heard Coleridge's voice, and saw him still holding onto the button, his arm outstretched, chatting "just as when I left him. He had never missed me."

John Keats met with him to see for himself the extent to which Coleridge had slipped from reality. He wrote to a friend of his encounter:

I walked with him, at his alderman-after-dinner pace, for near two miles, I suppose. In those two miles he broached a thousand things. Let me see if I can give you a list—Nightingales—Poetry—on Poetical sensation—Metaphysics—Different genera and species of Dreams—Nightmare—a dream accompanied with a sense of touch—single and double touch—a dream related—First and second consciousness—the difference explained between will and Volition—so say mathematicians from a want of smoking the second consciousness—Monsters—the Kraken—Mermaids —Southey believes in them—Southey's belief much too diluted—a Ghost story—Good morning—I heard his voice as he came towards me—I heard it as he moved away—I heard all the interval—if it may be called so.

• • •

WRITERS have always had their heroes—for inspiration, for influence, for pleasure, and, sometimes, for material. Samuel Taylor Coleridge said that *Oedipus Tyrannus*, *The Alchemist*, and *The History of Tom Jones* were the three most perfect plots ever conceived. F. Scott Fitzgerald advised young readers to peruse Dostoyevsky's *The Brothers Karamazov*, to "see what the novel can do," but listed *Madame Bovary*, *Vanity Fair*, and Joseph Conrad's *Nostromo* among his favorites. John Galsworthy, a passenger aboard the *Torrens*, encountered a young Polish sailor. They spoke frequently, and Galsworthy delighted in his companionship, saying, "He has a fund of yarns on which I draw fully." The sailor adopted English as his "first" language in his forties, changed his name from Teodor Jozef Konrad Korzeniowski to Joseph Conrad, and started his own career as a writer, using his fund of stories himself.

. . .

SAMUEL Taylor Coleridge said that material is borrowed from writer to writer and from generation to generation, "in a series of imitated imitations—shadows of shadows of shadows of a farthing-candle placed between two looking glasses."

. . .

SOME authors have had to overcome more than writing blocks or a new word processor. Lady Jane Grey, for example, ruled as England's queen for nine days when Edward VI died. When Edward's half-sister, Mary I, took the throne away from her, she banished Lady Jane, only seventeen, to the Tower of London during her trial. She was offered a pardon if she renounced her faith and became a Catholic. She refused and was immediately beheaded. In her jail cell were found pieces of paper covered in tiny pinpricks. It was later discovered that, when held to the light, the marks formed verses she had composed before her death.

. . .

ONE of the biggest best-sellers of all time featured an acknowledgment from the author to a friend who later shot and killed him. The author was Dr. Herman Tarnower, the book was *The Complete Scarsdale Diet*, and the friend was Jean Harris.

M ANY writers avoid deadlines the way a cat shuns water. One such writer is Ed McClanahan, whose autobiographical novel, then titled, *From a Considerable Height,* was signed by the Dial Press in 1962. He had a series of editors, including Christopher Lehmann-Haupt, E. L. Doctorow, and Henry Robbins. "I kept editors at arm's length," McClanahan explained. When Delacorte took over Dial in 1969, the novel was dropped and picked up by Farrar, Straus and Giroux. A new platoon of editors was assigned to the project, and they had no more luck than their predecessors at Dial. In 1980, Pat Strachan issued an ultimatum: McClanahan had one year—or else. Under the gun, McClanahan obliged, and twenty-one years after the contract was signed, the novel, retitled, *The Natural Man,* was published to resounding success.

• • •

I N a letter to his brother, Oliver Goldsmith warned him about letting his young nephew read novels. "These paint beauty in colours more charming than nature; and describe happiness that man never tastes . . . take my word for it that books teach us very little of the world."

• • •

E LIZABETH Hardwick preached the opposite, saying that reading gave her much joy as well as "friends who care for the same things. . . . The greatest gift is the passion for reading. It is cheap, it consoles, it distracts, it excites, it gives you knowledge of the world and experience of a wide kind. It is a moral illumination."

ON a trip to his beloved Paris, Benjamin Franklin was asked by his hostess to participate in a parlor game in which her guests would each contribute an answer to a specific question. The question was, "What condition of man most deserved pity?" Franklin thought for a moment and responded, "A lonesome man on a rainy night who does not know how to read."

• • •

JOHN Updike sees the reader as a safe harbor in an unforgiving sea. "Writers take words seriously—perhaps the last professional class that does—and they struggle to steer their own through the crosswinds of meddling editors and careless typesetters and obtuse and malevolent reviewers in to the lap of the ideal reader."

• • •

IN 1870, *The American Woman's Home* was published. It was a hefty volume containing all sorts of advice for the newly married woman who was setting up her household. One of the pieces of wisdom warned the American woman against "excessive mental action" that "wastes time and energies, [and] undermines the vigor of the nervous system." The authors criticized "novel-reading and castle-building" as wasteful—even harmful—pastimes. "Any one who has read the misanthropic wailings of Lord Byron has seen the necessary result of great and noble powers bereft of their appropriate exercise, and, in consequence, becoming sources of the keenest suffering."

The authors of the book were sisters—Catharine Beecher and Harriet Beecher Stowe; the latter was the first

American author to sell over a million copies of her novel, *Uncle Tom's Cabin*.

Lord Byron may have answered the Beecher sisters with a reference to a letter he penned to a friend:

> I have never courted the public and will never yield to it. As long as I can find a *single* reader I will publish my Mind (while it lasts) and write whilst I feel the impetus. As to profit, that is another matter—if none is to be attained—it must be dispensed with. Profit or loss—they shall never subdue me while I keep my senses.

• • •

THERE is no hard and fast rule regarding the size or invincibility of the writer's ego. Some egos are as fragile as wet tissue paper, while others have the solidity of reinforced steel. Aware of his colleague's sturdy ego, William F. Buckley sent Norman Mailer a copy of his latest book. Instead of inscribing the flyleaf, Buckley simply wrote, "Hi" next to Mailer's name in the index.

George Bernard Shaw did not mince comparisons when he said, "With the single exception of Homer, there is no eminent writer, not even Sir Walter Scott, whom I can despise so entirely as I despise William Shakespeare when I measure my mind against his." Thornton Wilder was only a fraction subtler. "I think I write in order to discover on my shelf a new book which I would enjoy reading, or to see a new play that would engross me." Ford Madox Ford acknowledged, "I learned all I know of Literature from [Joseph] Conrad—and England has learned all it knows of Literature from me."

James Thurber tells a story of visiting the home of Frank Harris. Prominently displayed were three portraits—one of Mark Twain and one of what Thurber thought to be Nathaniel Hawthorne, flanking one of Harris himself. Harris noticed Thurber admiring the paintings and said, "Those three are the best American writers. The one in the middle is best."

Jane Austen was less convinced of her talent. She wrote, "I think I may boast myself to be with all possible vanity, the most unlearned and uninformed female who ever dared to be an authoress."

In a rather uncharacteristic display of humility, Ernest Hemingway admitted, "I have tried simply to write the best I can; sometimes I have good luck and write better than I can."

In the March 1887 issue of *The Atlantic Monthly,* Agnes Repplier wrote of Sir Walter Scott's modesty when it came to self-criticism:

> [He] who was strangely disposed to undervalue his own merit as a poet, preserved the most genuine enthusiasm for the work of others. When his little daughter was asked by James Ballantyne [Scott's literary manager] what she thought of *The Lady of the Lake,* she answered with perfect simplicity that she had not read it. "Papa says there is nothing so bad for young people as reading bad poetry."

WHEN writers talk of fellow writers, they rarely fence-sit. Alfred Lord Tennyson, for example, said of Swinburne, "[He] is a reed through which all things blow music." John Ruskin was also a great admirer of Swinburne: "He simply sweeps me away before him as a torrent does a pebble." While Tennyson touted Swinburne, W. H. Auden touted Tennyson: "He had the finest ear, perhaps, of any English poet; he was also undoubtedly," Auden specified, "the stupidest; there was very little about melancholia he didn't know; there was little else he did."

Critiquing the literary forebears and contemporaries, certain writers dipped their pens liberally into the inkwell of poison. Commenting on *Measure for Measure*, Samuel Taylor Coleridge said, "A hateful work, although Shakespearian throughout."

Edmund Wilson remarked on Carl Sandburg winning the 1939 Pulitzer Prize for his biography of Abraham Lincoln, "The cruelest thing that has happened since he was shot by Booth has been to fall into the hands of Carl Sandburg."

Reviewing *Robinson Crusoe*, Stephen Spender wrote, "An English book, and only the English could have accepted it as adult literature: comforted by feeling that the life of adventure could be led by a man duller than themselves. No gaiety, wit or invention"

Anthony Trollope wrote that *War and Peace* had "absolutely no plot—no contrived arrangement of incidents by which interest is excited." After reading Thomas Wolfe's first novel, *Look Homeward Angel*, F. Scott Fitzgerald wrote a note to Max Perkins, the editor the two writers shared and the person to whom the book had been dedicated: "I liked the dedication, but after that I thought it fell off a bit."

D. H. Lawrence was not overly fond of James Joyce's *Ulysses*, which he read upon its publication in 1922. "My God, what a clumsy *olla putrida* James Joyce is. Nothing but old fags and cabbage stumps of quotations from the Bible and the rest, stewed in the juice of deliberate, journalistic dirty-mindedness."

After being misquoted, Robert Browning, in a letter to a friend, clarified his comment on Lord Byron:

> In the *Spectator* which came yesterday, somebody repeated that foolish lie that I called Lord Byron "a flatfish" . . . I never said nor wrote a word against Byron's poetry or power in my life; but I did say, that, if he were in earnest and preferred being with the sea to associating with mankind, he would do well to stay with the sea's population.

• • •

HONORÉ de Balzac liked to write between midnight and dawn, drinking cup after cup of coffee. He finally did succumb to caffeine poisoning and, lying on his death-bed, looked up at the doctor tending him and demanded he send for Dr. Bianchon. The doctor was confused and asked Balzac's friends who this mysterious Dr. Bianchon was, and why Balzac preferred Bianchon to him. The doctor was only slightly reassured to be told that Dr. Bianchon was a character in Balzac's *La Comédie Humaine*. The dying writer wanted his own creation to tend to him during his final hours.

R AYMOND Chandler, unamused by a glowing profile of Ernest Hemingway in *The New Yorker*, said, "I realize that I am much too clean to be a genius, much too sober to be a champ, and far, far too clumsy with a shotgun to live the good life."

• • •

T WO very different writers discussing the same character expressed the same sentiment very differently. Aldous Huxley wrote of Charles Dickens's popular Little Nell: "The history of Little Nell is distressing indeed, but not as Dickens presumably meant it to be distressing; it is distressing in its ineptitude and vulgar sentimentality." Oscar Wilde summed up Huxley's sentiments with the simple and accurate swipe: "One must have a heart of stone to read the death of Little Nell by Dickens without laughing."

• • •

O F Goethe's *Faust*, G. H. Lewes wrote, "It appeals to all minds with the irresistible fascination of an eternal problem, and with the charm of endless variety. It has every element: wit, pathos, wisdom, farce, mystery, melody, reverence, doubt, magic and irony: not a chord of the lyre is unstrung, not a fibre of the heart untouched."

• • •

L ITERARY kinships, friendships, pen pals, mentors, and lovers have had all manner of influences on all types of books. A young poet, on the occasion of the publication of a volume of poems, received a fan letter from Robert Browning and wrote to a friend, "I had a letter from Browning, the poet, last night, which threw me into ecstasies—Browning, the author of *Paracelsus, the King of the Mystics.*" So enraptured, the poet then wrote back to Browning:

> I will say that I am your debtor, not only for this cordial letter and for those all the pleasure which came with it, but in other ways, and the highest: and I will say that while I live to follow this divine art of poetry, in proportion to my love for it, I must be a devout admirer and student of your works. This is in my heart to say to you—and I say it.

The "devout admirer and student" was Browning's future wife, Elizabeth Barrett.

• • •

SOMERSET Maugham gave a begrudging tip of his hat to Jane Austen's enduring popularity. "Nothing very much happens in her books, and yet, when you come to the bottom of the page, you eagerly turn it to learn what will happen next. Nothing very much does and again you eagerly turn the page. The novelist who has the power to achieve this has the most precious gift a novelist can possess." Amen.

• • •

EDMUND Wilson, discussing Sir Arthur Conan Doyle, wrote:

> My contention is that Sherlock Holmes is literature on a humble not ignoble level. . . . The old stories are literature, not because of the conjuring tricks and the puzzles, not because of the lively melodrama . . . but by virtue of imagination and style. These are fairy-tales,

as Conan Doyle intimated in his preface to his last collection, and they are among the most amusing of fairy-tales and not among the least distinguished.

• • •

I N a letter to Raymond Chandler, Ian Fleming took a self-effacing stand when he wrote:

> Probably the fault about my books is that I don't take them seriously enough and meekly accept having my head ragged off about them in the family circle. . . . You, after all, write "novels of suspense" . . . if not sociological studies—whereas my books are straight pillow fantasies of the bang-bang, kiss-kiss variety.

• • •

J AMES Laughlin, the founder of New Directions, de- scribed a close call involving the works of E. M. Forster. "Owing to a tiff over an invitation to lunch in London, . . . Knopf had allowed the Forster books to go out of print, so we were able to lease two of those from him." Lionel Trilling, at Laughlin's urging, wrote a book about Forster that greatly helped bring Forster back into the popular mainstream.

The same fate nearly nicked F. Scott Fitzgerald. Although extremely popular early in his career, at the time of his death in 1940, not one of Fitzgerald's novels was in print. Edmund Wilson pulled together an eclectic collection of Fitzgerald's shorter pieces written late in life, and this helped sustain a rediscovery of his work. The collection was titled *The Crack-Up* and went through five printings, prompting Scribner's to reissue all of Fitzgerald's works.

H ANS Christian Andersen made detailed plans for his funeral. He asked the friend who was composing the funeral march to keep an important element in mind as he wrote. "Most of the people who will walk after me will be children, so make the beat keep time with little steps."

• • •

W HEN Dorothy Parker went to pay her last respects to F. Scott Fitzgerald, who lay in an undertaker's parlor in Hollywood, she could only shake her head and say aloud, "The poor son-of-a-bitch." These are the words spoken by a nameless mourner at the funeral of Jay Gatsby.

• • •

L AURENCE Sterne, the author of *Tristram Shandy*, died alone, and only his bookseller, Becket, was in attendance at his burial. Some weeks later, during an anatomy lesson at Cambridge University, the horrified students recognized the late writer, and the cadaver was returned to the graveyard for reburial.

• • •

T HE Pulitzer Prize for fiction, the most prestigious literary award in the United States, has twice been awarded posthumously. The first time was in 1958, when it was given to James Agee for *A Death in the Family*. Then, in 1981, the award was given in honor of John Kennedy Toole—twelve years after he had committed suicide and seventeen years after completing the work. Toole had written his only novel, *A Confederacy of Dunces*, while in the army. In 1969, depressed because he could not find a publisher, he took his own life. His mother, Thelma, sent the tattered manuscript to other publishers—again without success. Finally, in 1976, she took the novel to novelist Walker Percy, who persuaded Louisiana State University Press to publish the work. It became the press's first national best-seller.

• • •

DANTE Gabriel Rossetti, so profoundly grieved by his young wife's suicide (she took an overdose of laudanum), took copies of his poetry and laid them in her arms before the coffin was sealed. Most of his work had been inspired by his beloved Elizabeth, and he wanted it to go through all eternity with her. However, as the wounds healed, Rossetti came to regret his romantic gesture. His best works were lost to the dust of the grave. He finally was able to secure permission to dig up the coffin and retrieve the poetry. The poems were published (with some additions) in 1870, and *Poems* became an immediate best-seller.

• • •

SOPHOCLES wrote enthusiastically, to the point of neglecting daily chores like paying bills and generally managing his considerable property. His sons forced him to stand trial, expecting a jury to pronounce him senile and, therefore, incompetent so they could take over the estate. Sophocles, in an effort to prove himself perfectly capable, recited in the courtroom his play *Oedipus at Colonus*, which he had just completed. After his spirited reading, the judge and jury proclaimed him perfectly sound of mind and body, and he was freed to return to his writing and his land.

IN his late seventies, approaching death, Ralph Waldo Emerson realized his memory was leaving him. Suffering from what is now recognized as Alzheimer's disease, Emerson fought off the confusion and resisted the loss by sticking labels onto everything, describing their function because the names became meaningless. For example, "the thing that strangers take away," was pinned to his umbrella. Attending Longfellow's funeral, he whispered to a friend, "That gentleman had a sweet, beautiful soul, but I have entirely forgotten his name."

• • •

HAVING recently graduated from The Citadel, a group of former cadets decided to write a novel, a tribute to a particular colonel at the academy nicknamed The Boo. The group put up $1,500 to have *The Boo*, written by one of the young men, published by a Charleston printer. Then, some seventeen years ago, literary agent Julian Bach received a phone call. The deep, nervous voice belonged to the fledgling writer calling from a tiny island off the Carolina coast. Haltingly, the writer described his second novel. Bach was intrigued and asked to see the manuscript. The agent fondly recalls the moment he settled in to read the work. By the eleventh page, he felt a tear fall and knew this young man was "a born writer." He submitted the novel to Houghton Mifflin. The editor called ten days later to offer a $7,500 advance and standard royalties. Delighted, Bach called his client to report the good news that Houghton Mifflin wanted the book for $7,500. There was, recalls Bach, "a titanic silence" and then the writer stammered that he couldn't possibly afford to pay that much. Bach happily explained that the publisher paid the writer and not the other way around. The author was Pat Conroy and *The Water is Wide* was the first in a series of successes which includes *The Lords of Discipline* (in which the Boo appears as the Bear), *The Great Santini,* and *The Prince of Tides.*

• • •

THE following epitaph was suggested by Benjamin Franklin for his own gravestone and is now used to close our book:

The Body of
B. Franklin, Printer
(Like the cover of an old book,
Its contents torn out,
And Stript of its Lettering and Gilding)
Lies here, Food for Worms.
But the Work shall not be Lost;
For it will (as he believ'd) appear once more,
In a new and more elegant Edition
Corrected and amended
By the Author.